Cambridge Elements ≡

Elements in Shakespeare and Pedagogy
edited by
Liam E. Semler
The University of Sydney
Gillian Woods
University of Oxford

SHAKESPEARE AND NEURODIVERSITY

Laura Seymour
Birkbeck, University of London

CAMBRIDGE
UNIVERSITY PRESS

CAMBRIDGE
UNIVERSITY PRESS

Shaftesbury Road, Cambridge CB2 8EA, United Kingdom

One Liberty Plaza, 20th Floor, New York, NY 10006, USA

477 Williamstown Road, Port Melbourne, VIC 3207, Australia

314–321, 3rd Floor, Plot 3, Splendor Forum, Jasola District Centre, New Delhi – 110025, India

103 Penang Road, #05–06/07, Visioncrest Commercial, Singapore 238467

Cambridge University Press is part of Cambridge University Press & Assessment, a department of the University of Cambridge.

We share the University's mission to contribute to society through the pursuit of education, learning and research at the highest international levels of excellence.

www.cambridge.org
Information on this title: www.cambridge.org/9781009295949

DOI: 10.1017/9781009295932

When citing this work, please include a reference to the DOI 10.1017/9781009295932

First published 2025

A catalogue record for this publication is available from the British Library

ISBN 978-1-009-29594-9 Paperback
ISSN 2632-816X (online)
ISSN 2632-8151 (print)

Shakespeare and Neurodiversity

Elements in Shakespeare and Pedagogy

DOI: 10.1017/9781009295932
First published online: January 2025

Laura Seymour
Birkbeck, University of London

Author for correspondence: Laura Seymour, laura.seymour@bbk.ac.uk

ABSTRACT: Shakespeare and Neurodiversity argues that the Shakespeare classroom should be a place where neurodivergent learners flourish. This Element addresses four key areas: questions of reasonable adjustments, the pace of learning, the issue of diagnosis, and Shakespearean neurodivergent futures in education. Throughout, the Element provides activities and theoretical explanations to enable students and educators to understand how these four areas of Shakespeare education have often been underpinned by ableism, but can now become sources of neurodivergent flourishing.

KEYWORDS: shakespeare, neurodivergence, neurodiversity, pedagogy, neuroqueer

ISBNs: 9781009295949 (PB), 9781009295932 (OC)
ISSNs: 2632-816X (online), 2632-8151 (print)

Contents

Introduction

Clear Summary

- *Neurodiversity* means the natural variations in the ways human beings think and behave.
- *Neurodivergent* people often think and behave in a way that is different from the norm.
- The *neurodiversity paradigm* means accepting and celebrating these differences.
- It is likely that all classrooms are neurodiverse communities, with neurodivergent students in them.
- This Element is about how educators can help neurodivergent students to flourish.

Schooling Hotspur

In *Henry IV Part 1*, the English nobleman Harry Hotspur complains about the Welsh leader Owen Glendower. Hotspur protests that Glendower talks too much and that he enumerates too many (to Hotspur) irrelevant details in the process. Among Hotspur's complaints about Glendower is this experience:

> He held me last night at least nine hours
> In reckoning up the several devils' names
> That were his lackeys. I cried 'Hum', and 'Well, go to!'
> But marked him not a word.[1]

With what may be a deliberate exaggeration of how long he has been listening to Glendower, Hotspur objects to the temporality of Glendower's

---

[1] William Shakespeare, *The First Part of King Henry IV*, ed. Judith Weil and Herbert Weil (Cambridge: Cambridge University Press, 2007), III.i.150–54. Some editors replace 'But' with 'And'. Where an edition of a play is cited more than once, all subsequent references to that play are to the edition cited. I use Shakespeare's spelling, 'Owen Glendower', because I am referring to Shakespeare's literary character. The historical person this character was based on was called Owain Glyndŵr.

speech, which he sees as non-normative. Instead of the to and fro and comparative brevity of 'normal' conversation, Glendower spends 9 hours or more monologuing on a single topic: listing the names of the devils that serve him. Hotspur's preference for *not* listening to long monologues seems diametrically opposed to Glendower's prolixity. Hotspur describes Glendower's way of speaking as 'skimble-skamble stuff': confused, incoherent rambling (III.i.148). As a result of this attitude, Hotspur does not listen to Glendower: he 'cried "Hum" . . . But marked him not a word', that is, made non-committal noises and ignored him. Hotspur and Glendower's allies Mortimer and Worcester intervene, praising Glendower and chastising Hotspur, and telling Hotspur to be more polite. 'In faith', Mortimer states, 'he is a worthy gentleman' (III.i.159). Hotspur replies, 'Well, I am schooled' (III.i.184).

Hotspur raises the key question of this Element: what does it mean to be schooled in and by Shakespeare about different ways of communicating, thinking, and being? This generates new questions: what if instead of crying 'Hum' and ignoring people who don't think or behave in normative ways we listen to them and encourage their ways of thinking and behaving? What if we create classrooms that simultaneously accommodate the perspectives of people like Hotspur and Glendower, each of whose interactional needs and preferences seem so different to their comrade's? This Element is founded on the presupposition that it is desirable to celebrate students' different ways of engaging with Shakespeare. I examine how embracing and encouraging ways of thinking that are neurodivergent – different from neuro-norms – can generate new understandings of Shakespeare and enable neurodiverse classrooms not simply to exist but to flourish. A neurodiversity-inclusive classroom is crucial for Shakespeare studies, and crucial for the welfare of learners. Taught inclusively, Shakespeare's works can be a political tool that enables students and educators to understand and critique ableism in academia, and imagine new ways of teaching and learning.

What Is (Shakespearean) Neurodiversity?

Neurodiversity means the natural variations in the ways people think and behave, compared to each other. As Nick Walker explains, embracing neurodiversity as a paradigm for understanding humanity means refusing to pathologise certain ways of thinking and behaving as 'wrong', and refusing to subscribe to the notion that there is such a thing as a 'normal' person whose way of thinking and behaving is more correct, natural, or human than others':

> The dubious assumption that there is such a thing as a 'normal person' lies at the core of the pathology paradigm. The neurodiversity paradigm, on the other hand, does not recognise 'normal' as a valid concept when it comes to human diversity.[2]

Nobody owns the concept of neurodiversity, but it has a history shaped by specific people, and (hopefully) a future where neurodivergent people will lead its generative (re-)shaping and development. As Monique Botha, Morénike Giwa Onaiwu, Robert Chapman, Steven Kapp, Abs Stannard Ashley, and Nick Walker write, the concepts of neurodiversity and its synonym neurological diversity were 'collectively developed by neurodivergent people', with online autistic communities playing a significant role, and thus have 'multiple origins'.[3] Kassiane Asasumasu is credited with coining the terms 'neurodivergent' and 'neurodivergence' in 2000, to describe people whose ways of thinking and behaving differ from what society deems normal. The authors in *Neurodiversity Studies: A New Critical Paradigm* (2020), edited by Anna Stenning, Hanna Bertilsdotter Rosqvist, and Nick Chown, explore the ways in which the neurodiversity paradigm applies in academic contexts. The concept of neurodiversity has been shaped in various ways; for example, Athena Lynn Michaels-Dillon, Remi Yergeau, and Walker developed the practice of 'neuroqueering', which I discuss in Section 3. To give another example, Walker uses the term 'neurocosmopolitan' to mean engaging with neurodiversity in the same respectful and open way that we ought to approach cultural diversity; just as

---

[2] Nick Walker, *Neuroqueer Heresies* (Fort Worth, TX: Autonomous Press, 2021), 23.

[3] Monique Botha, Morénike Giwa Onaiwu, Robert Chapman, et al., 'The Neurodiversity Concept Was Developed Collectively: An Overdue Correction on the Origins of Neurodiversity Theory', *Autism* 28(6) (2024), 1–4.

no one culture is superior to another, she explains, no one mind is superior to another.[4] Collective knowledge and respect for individuals' differences have been crucial to the development of the concepts of neurodiversity, neurodivergence, neuroqueering, and neurocosmopolitanism. Talking about neurodiversity in the Shakespeare classroom should likewise involve an emphasis on the knowledge students and educators can create and share collectively, respecting each others' different perspectives on Shakespeare and on neurodiversity itself.

In this Element, I use 'neurodivergent' to refer to people whose ways of thinking and behaving differ from society's norms. However, I use the word 'divergence' without upholding the validity of the norms we diverge *from*. Because this Element combats ableist norms that are present in the classroom, I often find it helpful to think about what these norms are and to suggest ways we might diverge from these norms. Even so, we do not have to bring norms into our notion of 'neurodivergence' at all: we can understand it simply as recognising the way people differ from *each other*, taking paths that diverge from one another.[5] Given this Element's literary and creative theme, we can also understand neurodivergence as a neuro-'diversion', understanding diversion as playfulness, and an absorbing interest. Like other disability studies scholars, I use the term 'neurotypical' to mean people whose ways of thinking and behaving correspond with what society deems normal. Sometimes I use the names of particular conditions, like OCD, autism, ADHD, Tourette Syndrome, synaesthesia, Down Syndrome, dyslexia, voice hearing, stuttering, brain injuries, anxiety, and dyspraxia. Though (as I discuss throughout this Element), the notion of a 'neurodivergent condition' can be restrictive and overly dogmatic, the phrase 'neurodivergent condition' is often used in education systems. Thus, when context-appropriate (for instance, when I am discussing attitudes to labels and diagnosis) I use the phrase in this Element. People who are autistic, dyslexic, and so on can also be referred to as 'neurodivergent'. Being neurodivergent

---

[4] Nick Walker, 'Neuroqueering the Future', 2022 Interview https://neuroqueer .com/interview-neuroqueering-the-future/ [Accessed 28 January 2022].

[5] I am grateful to Joel Casey for the idea of a neurodivergent person 'taking a different path' from other people, rather than diverging from a norm.

is not limited to people diagnosed with a particular set of conditions. The term neurodivergent (or neuroqueer, neurominority, neurocosmopolitan) can speak to a wide variety of people, and I aim to avoid gatekeeping who can use the term. People who do not identify with these labels may still find useful the content of what writers like myself, Walker, Yergeau, and Stenning et al., say. In this Element, I discuss addiction as a form of neurodivergence, for example, because describing addiction in this way might be destigmatising for some people. This Element is designed to be open to many ways of understanding neurodiversity, and features exercises and resources that can be used by a variety of people. Whether neurodivergent or neurotypical, every human is part of neurodiversity, and my aim is to offer a text that has some use to all of us.

Though this Element draws on some scientific writings, it is not much concerned with the scientific bases of neurodiversity. I am primarily focused on how we can enable neurodiverse classrooms to understand Shakespeare in a literary way. For me, the most important factor regarding scientific work on neurodiversity (including the sciences behind diagnostic criteria) is whether it helps our students to understand Shakespeare. Whether or not a person has a formal diagnosis does not determine whether they can call themselves neurodivergent. As I discuss in Section 3, a person's race, class, gender, and LGBTQ+ status can affect if and when they are diagnosed, and what kind of (mis)diagnoses they receive. Diagnoses can be weaponised against people, like the many trans and gender non-conforming autistic people who are told by medical professionals, their families, and society, that autism is causing their gender 'confusion'.[6]

As I explore throughout this Element, Shakespeare directed much of his poetic, literary language to describing characters, thought-processes, and situations that differ from the norm. Discussing Shakespeare's engagement with what we now call neurodivergence can prompt students to consider the

---

[6] For a discussion of ableism and transphobia in conservative accounts of autistic trans people, see Shon Faye, *The Transgender Issue* (London: Penguin, 2021), 107–08. For a discussion of the interrelations between being autistic and trans, see Yenn Purkis and Wenn Lawson, *The Autistic Trans Guide to Life* (London: Jessica Kingsley, 2021).

ways in which the history of neurodivergence extends into the past, beyond
the first coinages of the terms 'neurodivergent' and 'neurodiversity'.
Concomitantly, students can stay productively alert to the ways in which
past and present descriptions of neurodivergence are in conversation with
each other, and similar to and different from each other. Literature can offer
ways of understanding neurodiversity that are more exciting and inventive
than diagnostic criteria, and Shakespeare's plays provide many examples
of this.

In *Two Gentlemen of Verona*, for example, Shakespeare describes love
changing a person's 'wits' or mental processes. Valentine tells Proteus,
'Love is your master, for he masters you'; Proteus responds, 'Yet writers
say; as in the sweetest Bud, | The eating canker dwells; so eating love |
Inhabits in the finest wits of all'.[7] We do not need to turn to science to
investigate whether love changes brain chemistry or analyse whether
Valentine's description matches any particular condition in the *Diagnostic
and Statistical Manual of Mental Disorders (DSM)* in order to understand
this passage. Taking Proteus' cue ('writers say . . . ') we can analyse this
description in literary terms, close reading Shakespeare's language rather
than derailing our discussion too quickly onto diagnostic language. Love is
a master and a canker; the latter could mean an infection (which masters
Proteus) or parasite. If a parasite, love is an exogenous entity, living
intimately in Proteus' wits. This parasite masters its host, suggesting that
Proteus' self is subordinated to invading love. Proteus leaves open whether
love destroys the wits or is responsible for making them particularly fine
(the former, Valentine responds). Proteus' metaphor renders the wits as
a sweet 'Bud': something furled tight with potential for a further flourishing
which may be helped by, hindered by, or done in conjunction with Love.
These observations open the way for a rich exploration of Shakespeare's
representation of mental states and processes in the play, and might be read
alongside Ian Frederick Moulton's analysis of how early modern concepts
of lovesickness which opposed love and reason are very different to twenty-
first-century assumptions that 'there is a self-evident connection between

[7] William Shakespeare, *Two Gentlemen of Verona*, ed. Kurt Schlueter with
     Lucy Munro (Cambridge: Cambridge University Press, 2012), I.i.39, 42–44.

love and happiness'.[8] In Shakespeare's time, Moulton explains, love was often situated in the realm of disability and lovesickness was 'a serious medical condition . . . a wasting disease'.[9] Though it is useful to note that Valentine's 'canker' activates the realm of the medical, I argue that we should draw on scientific writings and diagnostic criteria only when they genuinely help us to make sense of our world and Shakespeare's place in it. This Element, then, argues for the importance of reading and literature to neurodiversity: how we can read Shakespeare neurodivergently and read Shakespearean neurodivergence.

Returning to Glendower and Hotspur's complaints about his nine-hour-long list of devils' names: Mortimer and Worcester base their acceptance of Glendower on his aristocratic maleness and martial prowess. To his statement that Glendower is 'a worthy gentleman', Mortimer adduces the fact that Glendower has read a lot, is friendly and likeable, is brave in battle, and knows about the occult, linking this praise to an exoticised 'India' which suggests colonial activity:

> In faith, he is a worthy gentleman,
> Exceedingly well read, and profited
> In strange concealments, valiant as a lion
> And wondrous affable, and as bountiful
> As mines of India (1 *Henry IV*, III.i.159–163)

A fundamental concept of disability studies is that disabled lives are worthy in and of themselves. A disabled and/or neurodivergent person does not need to be particularly 'well read', high born, or 'wondrous affable' in order to be equal in worth to other human beings. In linking Glendower to the occult ('strange concealments'), Mortimer reflects the way in which Glendower frequently vaunts his own magical abilities and the supernatural omens surrounding his birth. Neurodivergence has historically been linked

---

[8] Ian Frederick Moulton, 'Catching the Plague: Love, Happiness, Health, and Disease in Shakespeare', in Sujata Iyengar, ed., *Disability, Health, and Happiness in the Shakespearean Body* (London: Routledge, 2014) (pp. 212–22), 212.

[9] Moulton, 'Catching the Plague', 215.

to the divine and supernatural (voice hearing, for example, can be both a religious and a neurodivergent experience), though all too often in a way that questions the humanity of neurodivergent people. 'Mines of India' may refer to the Indian subcontinent or to mining in the Americas; as Shankar Raman and the researchers on the TIDE Keywords project explain, 'India' was at the time a general placeholder for exoticism and 'fantastical' imaginings.[10] Mortimer's reference to bountiful India and emphasis on Glendower's capacity for violence adds to what Megan Lloyd identifies as the mix of foreign and familiar, and threatening and appealing, elements in Shakespeare's representation of Welsh characters.[11] Lloyd contends that Shakespeare's central purpose in doing so was to entertain his mainly English audiences. We might consider this alongside the ways in which neurodivergence can be represented for 'entertainment' on the Shakespearean stage, with author, actors, and directors combining a frisson of threat and alterity with 'human' touches in their portrayal of neurodivergent people. Worcester and Mortimer's biased praise of Glendower highlights the importance, in neurodivergent readings of any Shakespearean character, of bringing various factors into play (as here, references to social class, ethnicity, the supernatural, and gender), and researching the plays' historical context.

Reading This Element

Effective teaching in neurodiverse classrooms depends upon inclusive practices which *Shakespeare and Neurodiversity* aims to illustrate. With this in mind, I here indicate the various ways in which this Element may be used. The Element is divided into four sections, which build on each other but can also be read as standalone essays. Thus, the Element can be read all the way through in a linear fashion, or readers might navigate to a particular section

---

[10] See Shankar Raman, *Framing 'India': The Colonial Imaginary in Early Modern Culture* (Stanford, CA: Stanford University Press, 2001), 21, and 'Indian', in Nandini Das, João Vicente Melo, Lauren Working, et al., *Keywords of Identity, Race, and Human Mobility in Early Modern England* (Amsterdam: Amsterdam University Press, 2021), 143–47.

[11] Megan Lloyd, *Speak It in Welsh* (Plymouth: Lexington Books, 2007), 5, 149–50.

and read that by itself. Descriptions of the sections are at the end of this Introduction. Each section begins with a simple summary of its key ideas.[12] Each section is divided into shorter sub-sections, so one option is for readers to take breaks at these points.

This Element is designed to be a practical guide for teaching, so I hope that readers will take the activities I have recommended (several of which are inspired by other scholars and theatre professionals such as the acting coach Petronilla Whitfield), adapt them, and use them in the classroom. These exercises aim to stimulate the four habits of learning that Ayanna Thompson and Laura Turchi have argued twenty-first century advanced learners value: 'Participation in informal learning communities[,]Explicit explorations of identity[,] Following divergent paths to knowledge', and 'Innovative performances of their knowledge'.[13] I encourage readers to take what they need from my discussions and read it in the way that suits them best. There is a toolkit of resources at the end of the Element so that readers can find further explanations of the key issues I discuss.

There is no one way to teach inclusively, and this Element should not be seen as an immobile framework. Rather, readers are encouraged to adapt the ideas and exercises presented here to work with their own thinking and practice. I encourage readers to maintain a critical eye on how my whiteness and other positionalities may be informing this work. For instance, I am cisgender and disabled in specific ways (autistic and physically disabled by cancer) but writing about the vast topic of neurodiversity and ableism in general.

Whom This Element Is For

This Element is for anyone who teaches Shakespeare, whether in schools, colleges, and other post-16 education, home-schooling, universities, prisons, Further Education institutions, and 1:1 tuition, whether they are responsible for designing whole degree programmes, modules and assessments, or going

---

[12] I here follow the example of Kirsty Liddiard's use of simple summaries in her academic work, *The Intimate Lives of Disabled People* (London: Routledge, 2018).

[13] Ayanna Thompson and Laura Turchi, *Teaching Shakespeare with Purpose* (London: Bloomsbury Arden, 2016), 4.

through schoolwork with their young person after class, or whether they teach a fortnightly hour-long class covering someone else's syllabus. Some educators have more power and resources than others to help make their whole institution inclusive, however (as I argue in Section 1) there is a huge amount that an educator can do in a single class in terms of making positive changes for students and encouraging moments of collective joy that build community. No prior knowledge of neurodiversity, diagnostic criteria, or neuroscience is required to read and use this Element. Srikala Naraian and Nicole Schlessinger conclude that 'rather than seeing [teachers] as "agents of change" we need to see them as "changing agents" who both change and are changed by the contexts within which they enact their commitments'.[14] Readers may find that who they are as a teacher will change positively thanks to neurodiversity-inclusive changes they make in class.

Why This Element Is Needed, and Why Shakespeare Can Help

Ableism is baked into academia. Ableist notions of what looks like and counts as intelligence and scholarly learning (e.g. verbal fluency, the ability to participate spontaneously in synchronous discussion, processing verbal or written information swiftly, memorising quotations, focusing on a single set task for extended periods) play a large part in this situation. Neurodivergent students may often live up to these ableist notions; we should be wary of using this fact as evidence that our system is working or that these people are not really neurodivergent, and of using this as a basis for valuing one neurodivergent student above others. Autism, for example, is associated with memory skills, the ability to focus on a single topic for a long time, and the desire to gain deep, detailed knowledge about a topic of interest. Such qualities might help autistic students when they are given projects where they can use these skills. This does not mean that the education system is perfect for all neurodivergent people, or that we should value autistic people more than others because their skills coincide with what their society and educational institution currently values. A general atmosphere

---

[14] Srikala Naraian and Nicole Schlessinger, *Narratives of Inclusive Teaching: Stories of Becoming in the Field* (Oxford: Peter Lang, 2021), 158.

of ableism, and a failure to care holistically for these students' neurodivergence will still demoralise and hamper students (for instance, if said autistic student's sensory sensitivities are not addressed, or they are forced to witness their dyslexic friends get repeatedly crushed by ableist teaching, or their co-occurring conditions are not taken into account). Many neurodivergent students will not live up to existing norms. Take, for example, a student with ADHD who has a brilliant mind and the ability to achieve highly when they can bounce ideas around in dialogue with others and make generative connections between different topics, but who finds a three-hour exam in which they must sit still and write about a single topic inaccessible. Moreover, such factors intersect with other disadvantages students face in terms of race, gender, and socioeconomic status. Nicole Brown and Jennifer Leigh have amassed numerous examples of ableism in academia for staff members, which I draw on in Section 1.

Making education more inclusive for neurodivergent students can help everyone, including neurotypical students. For example, say an autistic student needs key points written down and visibly marked in bold text as important (as those with autism cannot always pick out what other people intend to be the 'key' information in a set of verbal instructions) and deadlines emphasised. This practice will no doubt help many other students to plan their time and understand what is happening in class. Imagine a world where institutions funded an alternative exam format to a student with ADHD that enables them to engage in dialogue with examiners rather than sitting and writing for three hours: this may suit the learning styles of other students too. Students with autism, dyslexia, and anxiety who need time to prepare might ask us to provide reading in advance, but surely this is helpful for everyone! When a request from one student with PTSD leads us to include trigger warnings for certain topics discussed in class, we may never know how many other students are helped thereby. As I argue in section 1, combatting ableism goes beyond simply making adjustments, however. It is about positively encouraging neurodiverse classrooms, and every member within them, to thrive.

Shakespeare studies is a space where we can create anti-ableist models of pedagogy and community from which educators and students can benefit. Shakespeare's quasi-permanence on curricula makes Shakespeare studies well-positioned to help make neurodiversity a permanent consideration in the classroom. The wide range of neurodivergent characters in Shakespeare's works, and his status as both playwright and poet, offer students opportunities to analyse a variety of neurodiversities (from, I shall argue in sections 2 and 3, autistic readings of the Bastard in *King John* to discussions of Ophelia and suicidal ideation and intent). Neurodivergent people often arrive at our classes already shaken by negative experiences with educators; Shakespeare's exclusionary associations with elitism and whiteness can compound this negativity. Neurodivergent people can make Shakespeare their own, including if that mainly involves articulating precisely why they dislike him, and how he's been used to oppress them. The Shakespeare canon offers students opportunities to consider engagements with literature that include devising neurodiversity-inclusive editing practices, exploring neurodiversity through performance, and analysing representations of neurodiversity in particular characters. This range of possibilities enables students to address key topics in Shakespeare studies – from textual editing to performance – in their own neurodiverse ways.

Sections in This Element

Section 1, 'There is neurodiversity in every classroom', discusses practical ways to adjust the classroom environment so that neurodivergent students cannot only access learning but can positively flourish. I argue that educators should not make adjustments with the aim of making neurodivergent students the same as everyone else, but rather should encourage students to express their neurodivergent ways of engaging with Shakespeare and to develop as learners in their own neurodivergent way. Section 2, 'No single way to read Shakespeare', explores what happens if we allow ourselves as educators to be guided by neurodivergent thinking styles and temporalities rather than insisting that neurodivergent students conform to neurotypical learning patterns and milestones. Though this Element is primarily about teaching neurodivergent students, many of us educators are ourselves neurodivergent and thus already have lived experience of thinking in a neurodivergent way. Section 3, 'Shakespeare's neurodivergent characters: beyond diagnosis', examines Shakespearean characters whom students might deem to have neurodivergent experiences and conditions, like PTSD and voice-hearing. I argue that if educators do decide to discuss diagnostic criteria in class, we should do so in a critical and historically-attentive way. The concluding section, 'What's past is prologue: neurodiverse futures' argues for using our literary-critical skills to imagine new inclusive futures for Shakespeare studies.

Getting to Work

Mortimer chastises Hotspur, telling him that Glendower admirably restrains himself in Hotspur's company: he 'curbs himself even of his natural scope | When you come cross his humour' (*1 Henry IV*, III.i.165–6). Glendower is 'curbing' himself in various ways: masking his natural propensity to expound on his favourite topics, and being polite to Hotspur when Hotspur is rude to him.[15] Mortimer asks Hotspur to focus less on critiquing Glendower, and more on disciplining his own behaviour: 'my lord, you are too wilful-blame ... You must needs learn, lord, to amend this fault' (III.i.171, 174). According to Hotspur, Glendower talks too much and too tediously. According to Mortimer, Hotspur is too rude and blunt towards Glendower. Mortimer's reason is that Hotspur's discourteously headstrong ('wilful-blame') behaviour towards Glendower ill befits a nobleman (III.i.180–1). However, as I hope I have made clear in this introductory section, there other reasons Hotspur should not ask Glendower to 'curb' his behaviour just because it is different from other people's. Not least, we discover wonderful things when we make it safe for people to stop masking and hiding, and feeling ashamed of their difference. Rather than thinking of either Glendower or Hotspur as disruptive and challenging per se, we can

---

[15] Masking most often refers to autistic people concealing our natural autistic behaviours for the benefit of neurotypical people (e.g. spending exhausting weeks preparing our small talk ahead of social events and forcing ourselves to make eye contact once we are there). However, the term is applicable in any context where a neurodivergent person is hiding their natural ways of behaving because of neuro-ableism. Masking is not deceitful; it is a survival tactic which ironically can lead to suicidal thoughts. Some neurodivergent people mask – and thus conform outwardly to societal norms – more readily than others.

recognise how much extra work neurodivergent people have to do to control and mask their behaviour to conform to all society's norms regarding what politeness, intelligence, collegiality, and learning ought to look like. Our neurodivergent students have already been working overtime on this, many of them for their whole lives. Now it is time for *us* to get to work.

1 There Is Neurodiversity in Every Classroom

Clear Summary

- Currently, educational institutions are usually ableist: they are rigged to benefit neurotypical students.
- Thus, it is important to adjust the way we teach, in order to meet the needs of neurodivergent students.
- Disability adjustments should not be about making neurodivergent students the same as neurotypical students.
- Disability adjustments should be about enabling neurodivergent students to flourish in their own neurodivergent way.

Set Me Where You Stand

(Content: discusses attempted suicide)

In Act 4 of *King Lear*, Edgar makes a few adjustments for his father Gloucester, who wants to walk to the edge of the cliffs of Dover and end his life by jumping from them. Edgar has disguised himself as a mad beggar called Poor Tom. Earlier in the play, Lear's daughter Regan and her husband Cornwall invaded Gloucester's home and blinded him. In the guise of Poor Tom, Edgar offers himself as Gloucester's sighted guide, leading him to Dover and describing the terrain to him along the way. However, Edgar misdescribes the terrain to confuse Gloucester. Edgar's stated aim is to 'cure' Gloucester (presumably of his suicidal intent) and to thwart his suicide attempt.[16] This scene can be a way in for students to consider questions of power, care, cure, class, gender, selfhood, disguise,

---

[16] William Shakespeare, *The Tragedy of King Lear*, ed. Jay Halio (Cambridge: Cambridge University Press, 2020), IV.v.34.

honesty, and relationships (whether professional, familial, or friendly) that arise when one person makes adjustments for another. Reading this scene with students, the discussion might begin with some questions that prompt an exploration of these relationships: Does Edgar need to discombobulate Gloucester while helping him, or are there other ways he might have behaved? How do the characters think, act, and react, and why might this be? Considering this scene from *King Lear* with students early in a Shakespeare class or module can open out conversations about what it means to make adjustments, what good adjustments look like, what changes as a result of making adjustments, and what challenges and difficulties can arise in this process. I suggest discussing this scene early on because, no matter how conversant students are with Shakespeare, it invites them to draw on something that they are expert in: their own opinions, experiences, and impressions of the scene. By focusing the discussion on the Shakespeare scene rather than asking for general opinions about disability adjustments, a conversation about adjustments can take place in a way that is boundaried, exercises students' close reading skills, and does not put any pressure on them to reveal personal information about their own relationship to adjustments. Having analysed this scene, adjustments are something that have *already been spoken about* in class, hopefully making it easier for educators to invite students, when appropriate and safe, to talk about what *they* need.

Having set himself up as a knowledgeable guide conversant with 'Both stile and gate, horseway and footpath' (IV.i.56), Edgar offers to lead Gloucester to the edge of a cliff but takes him instead to a flat patch of ground, insisting that Gloucester ought to be able to hear the sea and sense inclined ground with his vestibular system:

GLOUCESTER:	When shall I come to th' top of that same hill?
EDGAR:	You do climb up it now. Look how we labour.
GLOUCESTER:	Methinks the ground is even.
EDGAR:	Horrible steep.
	Hark, do you hear the sea?
GLOUCESTER:	No, truly.
EDGAR	Why then, your other senses grow imperfect
	By your eyes' anguish.

GLOUCESTER:	So may it be indeed.
	Methinks thy voice is altered and thou speak'st
	In better phrase and matter than thou didst.
EDGAR:	Y'are much deceived; in nothing am I changed
	But in my garments.
GLOUCESTER:	Methinks y'are better spoken. (IV.vi.1–10)

Gloucester communicates his own accurate sensory impressions: that they are on flat, not hilly, ground, he cannot hear the sea, and Edgar's style of speech has changed from the 'mad' echolalic diction he had previously used. Edgar denies these experiences and tells Gloucester that because of his disability he is unable to perceive anything properly: 'your other senses grow imperfect | By your eyes' anguish'. Gloucester considers this idea, musing, 'so may it be indeed'. Claiming they have reached the cliff, Edgar continues to play on Gloucester's emotions and suicidal intent, spending thirteen lines emphasising how dizzily high they are, and how certain death would be, were Gloucester to jump (IV.v.11–24).

At the supposed cliff edge, Gloucester asks Edgar to help him to stand in the same position as him:

GLOUCESTER:	Set me where you stand.
EDGAR:	Give me your hand. You are now within a foot
	Of th' extreme verge. For all beneath the moon
	Would I not leap upright.
GLOUCESTER:	Let go my hand.
	Here, friend, 's another purse (IV.vi.24–28)

Gloucester's 'set me where you stand' and 'give me your hand' evoke requests for care and aid as he ends his life. Gloucester pays Edgar for this service, and when the time comes, he tells Edgar he does not need his caring or guiding touch any longer because this is the point at which he will die, 'Let go my hand'. As this is a crux in Gloucester and Edgar's interaction, it is a good moment to pause and ask students what kind of relationship the two characters have at this point. When Gloucester has 'jumped', Edgar reappears pretending to be a person lurking at the foot of the cliff and tells Gloucester he could only have survived his fall because his body is extremely insubstantial, like 'gossamer, feathers, air' (IV.vi.49). Edgar tells Gloucester that Gloucester's selfhood is, in Edgar's eyes, fragile. Edgar feels empowered to break Gloucester's selfhood down and build it back up again, as he tells Gloucester he now has 'heavy substance' (after his gossamer-like falling form) and his 'life's a miracle' (IV.vi.52, 56). Edgar informs us in an aside that he treats Gloucester in this way in order to 'cure him': 'Why I do trifle thus with his despair | Is done to cure it', IV.vi.33–4. Students might consider the extent to which love, dignity, care, and communication are at play in this scene and ask: what in the preceding scenes of the play has led the characters to this point? How does Edgar and Gloucester's interaction in IV.vi affect the rest of the play? Discussing the above passage may involve bringing difficult topics into the classroom, such as suicide and failures of care. These topics are already there in many of our students' life-experiences, so as with any potentially triggering topic educators can help students out by providing a content note for the class (as I did at the start of this section), emphasising that they can take a break from the discussion if they need to, and setting ground rules around respectful conversations. Ground rules might include:

- Not speaking on behalf of other students
- Keeping any personal disclosures that other students make confidential
- Not telling other people in the class that their experiences did not happen, or did not happen in the way they said. Instead, students who feel confused by something another student has said can ask 'can you tell me more about it?'

At the same time, considering Edgar and Gloucester's clifftop scene might prompt educators to ask difficult questions about their own practice. Edgar states that his 'trifling' with Gloucester 'is done to cure' his 'despair'. Educators should stay within their professional competency: it is unethical for educators to have curing (rather than teaching!) neurodivergent students as an aim. However, even when educators stay within their professional competency and training, do they ever find themselves pursuing such an aim? As Margaret Price discusses in *Mad at School*, many teaching methods are subtly and insidiously geared at correcting neurodivergent students' neurodivergence: getting them to speak, behave, and write 'properly' (i.e. in an abled way).[17] In this section, I ask, what if educators do not aim to 'cure' neurodivergent students, thereby making their selfhood invisible and diminished in the classroom ('gossamer, feathers, air')? What if, instead, educators decide that it is fundamental to their work to support these students honestly and caringly to flourish as their own, neurodivergent selves. What if, instead of using our power to make adjustments with great fanfare to demonstrate what good people we are, we focus on the students' needs without centring ourselves?

In his interaction with Gloucester on the imagined cliff, Edgar manipulates vocabularies and ideas of care and assistance, with fascinating results. Edgar is going through his own difficulties: he was banished from court after Edgar's half-brother Edmund told everyone that Edgar planned to assassinate their father, he replaced his fine clothes with dirty rags to maintain the pretence that he is Poor Tom, and spent at least one unpleasant stormy night with Lear and the Fool in a hovel. Edgar and Gloucester's care relationship is mutual, perhaps because on some level Gloucester has realised that his guide is his son Edgar, but also because Gloucester wants to help Poor Tom on a human level as another person with obvious needs. Gloucester asks a man that they pass if he can find some clothes for Edgar who is nearly naked, he gives Edgar money, and he prays for him in what he imagines will be one of his final acts. In the specific context of the classroom, Gloucester's phrase 'set me where you stand' might invite us to consider the issue of positionalities. In this phrase, the disabled character asks the able-bodied and potentially neurodivergent character to guide him so that he stands where the able-bodied man stands. Students might reflect on their embodied experience of the classroom: what can they see and hear from their position right now and how does it affect their learning? Examples of issues that might arise include: Can they see and/or hear as they would like to from their place? How free do they feel to move around? How close to

---

[17] Margaret Price, *Mad at School* (Ann Arbor, MI: Michigan University Press, 2011), 25–57. In the US context, Jay Dolmage traces the eugenic ideologies behind many teaching methods, *Academic Ableism: Disability and Higher Education* (Ann Arbor, MI: Michigan University Press, 2017).

the exit are they and how do they feel about this? Students and educators can also ask a more conceptual question about positionality: what if we do not consider ableism and the abled bodymind to be the guide and marker of where we all want to be? Bodymind is a phrase often used in disability studies to suggest that body and mind are interdependent: I embrace this concept in this Element.

In this section, I explore alternatives to simply setting neurodivergent students where neurotypical people are standing. Perhaps the place where neurotypical educators are standing is not an ideal location or destination. Instead of setting neurodivergent students where we stand, making the world discombobulating to them and denying their interpretations of it, we can listen to their interpretations, let them impact and shape their own environment and flourish in a place that they truly want to be. Making our classrooms neurodiversity-inclusive is about honestly examining our environment and the ground we stand on.[18]

Adjustments: As Fundamental as the Ground We Stand on

How is the terrain in the classroom? 'Horrible steep', or 'even'? In this section, I embrace a holistic notion of access, which is not just about access to the physical classroom space through adjustments like dyslexia-friendly fonts and clear autism-friendly structures (though these are key ingredients of accessibility) but which encompasses access to community, opportunities, comradeship, flourishing, joy, and creativity. As Leah Lakshmi Piepzna-Samarasinha describes in *Care Work: Dreaming Disability Justice*, disability justice is holistic, intersectional, communal, and, crucially, mutual. Rather than one person making adjustments and another receiving them, true disability justice involves what she calls 'care webs' of mutual, holistic support. She writes:

---

[18] This can intersect with the ways in which, in countries with a history of colonial violence, educators acknowledge whose stolen lands universities are built on, with whose money, and whose labour. Finding out, for those of us who are ignorant of this knowledge, about how Indigenous people theorise and describe disability and neurodiversity is a valuable part of such acknowledgement.

When I think about access, I think about love.

I think that crip solidarity, and solidarity between crips and non(yet)-crips is a powerful act of love and I-got-your-back. It's in big things, but it's also in the little things we do moment by moment to ensure that we all – in our individual bodies – get to be present fiercely as we make change.[19]

Providing an example, they write, 'If I'm having a pain day and a hard time processing language and I need you to use accessible language, with shorter words and easiness about repeating if I don't follow, and you do, that's love. And that's solidarity'.[20] We can include this love and solidarity in our classrooms.

It is inevitable that we will encounter neurodivergent students in our Shakespeare classrooms. The ADHD Institute estimate that globally 2.2–2.8 per cent of people have ADHD, whilst according to the WHO worldwide around 1 in 160 people are autistic (this varies by country, for instance the National Autistic Society estimates around 1 in 100 in the UK, on a par, Spectrum News reports, with recent figures from China whilst the CDC reports that autism diagnoses have been increasing in children in the USA reaching 1 in 36 children in 2020).[21] Estimates of dyslexia hover around

---

[19] Leah Lakshmi Piepzna-Samarasinha, *Care Work: Dreaming Disability Justice* (Vancouver: Arsenal Pulp Press, 2018), 75. Piepzna-Samarasinha's work has immense power to improve education institutions; however, they themselves are avowedly outside the academy. This raises the questions of what it means to apply their work in the context of this Element, and of the extent to which radical disability justice can ever be truly realised inside our educational institutions.

[20] Piepzna-Samarasinha, *Care Work*, 75. They conclude, 'Love gets laughed at. What a weak, non-political, femme thing. Love isn't a muscle or an action verb or a survival strategy. Bullshit, I say. Making space accessible as a form of love is a disabled femme of color weapon', *Care Work*, 78.

[21] adhd-institute.com/burden-of-adhd/epidemiology; who.int/news-room/fact-sheets/detail/autism-spectrum-disorders; autism.org.uk/advice-and-guidance/what-is-autism; spectrumnews.org/news/autism-prevalence-estimates-for-china-greece-align-with-global-patterns/; cdc.gov/ncbddd/autism/data.html [all accessed March 2023].

10 per cent worldwide, though the International Dyslexia Society notes that up to 20 per cent of people worldwide have a language-based learning disability.[22] These statistics do not tell a complete story. Many neurodivergent people do not receive a diagnosis because of sexism, transphobia, racism, and classism in the diagnostic process and/or because of long waiting lists, expensive healthcare, and additional stigma around their conditions. Writing of lived experience of cocaine and heroin addiction, for instance, Maia Szalavitz argues that addiction ought to be considered a form of neurodiversity as this would help to recognise the role of genetics, environment, and brain chemistry in addiction and reduce the stigma experienced by people with addictions.[23] Several neurodivergent people reject official diagnosis as an objective marker of identity and make an informed decision to eschew diagnosis altogether or to self-diagnose. Several make self-diagnoses that are later confirmed or contested by a professional. Thus, I do not lean heavily on statistics in this section, other than to note that it is statistically highly probable that we will teach several individuals with diagnoses of some neurodivergent condition, and moreover that we will have many individuals in our classes whose neuro-divergence is misdiagnosed or undiagnosed. Some neurodivergent people with diagnoses either partly or wholly reject their diagnosis; for example, they might accept that they are autistic but vehemently reject the DSM-V's description of autism as a 'deficit' (DSM-V abbreviates *Diagnostic and Statistical Manual of Mental Disorders*, 5th edition). Many neurodivergent people will never make it into our classrooms at all, or will leave education before their neurotypical peers do, because of ableism in society, teaching, and admissions processes. Regardless of whether a student has a diagnosis, and no matter how many doctors, friends and family members are providing us with information about the student's (potential) diagnosis, we should always centre what the student has to say about who they are and what they want. Rather than thinking of neurodivergent students in terms of

---

[22] https://dyslexiaida.org/frequently-asked-questions-2/ [accessed July 2022].

[23] Maia Szalavitz, *Unbroken Brain: A Radical New Way of Understanding Addiction* (New York: St Martin's Press, 2016). I am grateful to Azad Ashim Sharma for this reference.

percentages ('here's my class activity for the ~10 per cent of dyslexic students; here's something for the 1–2 per cent of autistic students'), I suggest that we use dialogue, solidarity, and engagement with our students to adjust our classrooms so that they work for our students in what I will describe as a holistically inclusive fashion.

Ableism in academia has many pernicious effects, including gaps in academic attainment and employability between disabled and non-disabled students. However, I suggest that we do not make adjustments with the main goal of making students more 'productive', getting them better grades, or having them speak up like a debating champion in class. These are markers of success stipulated by our imperfect educational systems and capitalist societies. Neurodivergent people are infinitely valuable just by *being*. Success can be a stuffy neurotypical concept, whilst failure can be (to adapt Jack Halberstam's LGBTQ+ focused celebration of 'the queer art of failure') a neuroqueer art.[24] Students will no doubt often achieve better, participate more, and work more 'productively' according to neurotypical standards when they have the adjustments they need. But this is not my end goal. Rather, my aim is to encourage students to be themselves, set their own goals, and flourish as and for themselves.

This section, then, does not merely recommend making reasonable adjustments so that neurodivergent people can simply participate in the same kinds of classrooms as are usual, with educators carrying on usual ableist ways of teaching. When the topic being taught is Shakespeare, it is particularly important to ensure that students are explicitly welcomed and included. Shakespeare is exclusionary and inaccessible on many fronts: his long-standing associations with whiteness, Englishness, and elite education mean that many students come to the Shakespeare classroom feeling that they are already on the periphery of Shakespeare studies. Making our classrooms neurodiversity-inclusive from the beginning enables us to disrupt these rigged and normative ways in which education works. It enables neurodivergent students to feel safe and welcome, and to develop in their

---

[24] I am creating a neurodivergent analogy to Jack Halberstam's discussion of success as a heteronormative concept in *The Queer Art of Failure* (Durham, NC: Duke University Press, 2010).

own, neurodivergent way rather than attempting to measure up to milestones and ways of learning that are not designed for their bodyminds. By teaching in the normal (rigged, ableist) way, and making adjustments (like dyslexia-friendly fonts) so neurodivergent people can attend our (rigged, ableist) classes, we often just enable neurodivergent people to access an ableist space. We simultaneously erase neurodivergence, make it invisible, as we adjust neuro-divergent students' learning so that it can blend in with dominant neurotypical learning styles. Nicole Brown calls this process 'striving for the absent body', an ableist way of rendering disabled people invisible in academic contexts that 'perpetuates the image of particular kinds of workers and workings, and thus the ableism that is so prevalent in academia'.[25] By asking neurodivergent staff and students to participate in this process, we ask them to participate in their own erasure. Laura Ellingson writes,

> The better we become at hiding our disabilities completely, or in over-functioning to provide industrious cover to our visible disabilities, the more we reinforce the ableist assumption that disabled scholars do not belong in the academy until or unless we can function without needing accommodations. This strengthens the idea that we also do not really need accommodations, given that at times we have managed to succeed despite their absence. Our resilience, creativity and exhaustion are taken as proof that there is nothing wrong with the status quo instead of evidence of the extra-ordinary lengths that we go to succeed and prove we can contribute positively to our universities.[26]

As the autistic poet Alex writes of neurotypical people in their poem 'Double Empathy, Empathy', 'I make adaptations for them every day |

---

[25] Nicole Brown, 'Introduction', in Nicole Brown, ed., *Lived Experiences of Ableism in Academia* (Bristol: Policy Press, 2021) (pp. 1–14), 6.

[26] Laura Ellingson, 'A Leg to Stand on: Irony, Autoethnography, and Ableism in the Academy', in Nicole Brown, ed., *Lived Experiences of Ableism in Academia* (Bristol: Policy Press, 2021) (pp. 17–36), 27.

And they never call them "reasonable adjustments"'.[27] Disabled staff
members' experiences of ableism (Ellingson's theme) is imbricated with
ableism experienced by students. If neurodivergent staff members mask and
make ourselves invisible this suggests to students either that there are no
neurodivergent staff members and thus neurodivergence precludes academic success, or that (if they notice our masking), that one must hide
one's neurodivergence in order to succeed. Paulo Freire reminds us that we
should change the mentality in education, so the oppressed do not simply
want to be like their oppressors.[28] Students may want any number of the
things their educators seem to have: an office, job stability, authority,
knowledge, money, a title and the perceived respect that comes with it.
All too often, ableism has enabled us to acquire these things. Brown reports
that UK graduate students are less likely than undergraduates to declare
their disabilities, perhaps because of their proximity to being a researcher or
educator themselves and thus to ableist ideas about what a researcher and
educator looks like.[29] However, I argue that we should not aim to make
students like us, but to fulfil their best potential on their own terms. When
we are ourselves at work, and when we explicitly value and celebrate
different ways of thinking, communicating, and behaving, we can inspire
students to be themselves.

One opposite of 'invisibility' for neurodivergent students is visibility.
However, visibility can be a poisoned chalice if handled badly; as Emma
Sheppard notes, when we make access an 'add on' for specific individuals,
'rather than a feature' of our classes from the start,

> access requires deliberate deviation from the standard pro-
> vision, often in ways which mark out the disabled person as

---

[27] Alex, 'Double Empathy, Empathy', in Janine Booth, Kate Fox, Rob Stevenson,
and Paul Neads (eds.), *NeurodiVERSE* (Manchester: Flapjack Press, 2022) (pp.
101–03), 101.

[28] 'In their alienation, the oppressed want at any cost to resemble the oppressors',
Paulo Friere, *Pedagogy of the Oppressed*, trans Myra Ramos (New York: Herder
& Herder, 1970), 62.

[29] Brown, 'Introduction', 3–4.

obviously different, and which reinforce the perception that this deviation is a form of special treatment. When the access requires a behavioural change or action(s) by others, this 'special treatment' becomes a burden to the others.[30]

Making access part of our business as usual, rather than a later addition to it, avoids this stigmatising and ostracising effect. Students do not experience access as an additional burden when it is taken care of from the start. When we emphasise that all students are being cared for as part of our 'business as usual' and set it up as a mutual, sustaining 'care web' rather than a set of isolated adjustments, students are less likely to find making adjustments for each other (e.g. putting their class presentations in a dyslexia friendly font) a burden but simply see this as part of belonging to a community from which they all benefit. Centring neurodivergent students' needs and acknowledging their positionalities helps to ensure that Shakespeare is accessible for all.

Holistic Access

Though I provide a template list of adjustments later in this section, it is crucial to talk to students regularly and asking about their *individual* needs. Asking students 'what do you need and prefer?' is generally more helpful than asking them 'what condition do you have?' Two students with the same condition, dyslexia, may have very different needs. No matter how clued-up we are about the access adjustments that meet different neurodivergent people's needs, we can never know what individual students need until we enable them to feel comfortable telling us. Asking students

---

[30] Emma Sheppard, '"I'm Not Saying This to Be Petty": Reflections on Making Disability Visible while Teaching', in Nicole Brown, ed., *Lived Experiences of Ableism in Academia* (Bristol: Policy Press, 2021) (pp. 185–96), 191. Sheppard focuses on staff asking students to make adjustments for them rather than the other way around, which brings different sets of expectations in to play (for instance, Sheppard suggests, students may feel they are not supposed to accommodate staff even though staff are supposed to accommodate them). However, Sheppard's arguments at this point hold true for both staff and students.

regularly what they need, and encouraging them to let us know when they need something new, is helpful because students' needs can change, for example some days students may have lower energy and may want to record the class rather than taking notes, whilst on other days they may be able to take notes for themselves. Students may discover more about themselves and their needs as time goes on. Perhaps they were diagnosed with autism and thought they should get a fidget toy because they saw other people with autism using them, only to later realise that the fidget toy isn't actually what they need. Asking students what they need is ineffective unless students know they are safe to express their needs. Students might have varying levels of confidence when it comes to talking about their neurodivergence with educators. Some students might have had traumatic experiences with educators in the past, and been shamed for their neurodivergence, making discussions about adjustments challenging for them. Educators can put students at ease, for example, by emphasising that making reasonable adjustments is a normal part of their job, and by regularly offering various opportunities for students to communicate about adjustments by email, individually in person, in class, and in an anonymous document (e.g., Google document). If a student writes anonymously on a Google document or discussion board 'please speak more slowly and clearly as I can't process your words when you speak so quickly', and in the next class the educator thanks the anonymous commenter for their request and speaks more slowly and clearly, students know that their adjustment requests are listened to.

Neurodivergence intersects with other aspects of students' identities like race, class, language, familiarity with Shakespeare, previous schooling, and individual temperament. When asking students what they need, educators can ask open questions like 'what do you need in order to learn well in class?' that are not explicitly focused on disability. Open questioning will often attract several neurodivergence-related responses, whilst enabling students to place their neurodivergence-related needs within a holistic picture. Such questions result in everything from students asking for particular fonts and dimmer lighting, to requests for anti-racist reading lists, to students saying that they give classmates permission to reign them in if they are dominating the discussion, to students revealing they get hungry at 11 am and need to have a snack at this point, or that the room is too cold for them to focus. Several writers on neurodiversity endorse this holistic approach to adjusting and shaping the classroom environment. Jenara Nerenberg suggests that we make 'temperament adjustments' in the workplace, social life, and education. Nerenberg explains,

> The idea of 'temperament rights' brings into the equation a consideration of our inner constitutions in every sphere of life—work, family, school, education, sports, religion, and more. The unique individual makeup of each person deserves its own articulation, respect, and corresponding accommodation. Note that this is not the same as every person getting exactly what they want all the time.[31]

Neurodiversity is sometimes described in terms of 'spiky profiles' which mean that while neurodivergence may give them difficulties in some areas, it will bring them strengths in others. For example, ADHD may be associated with difficulties with time management and particular strengths in empathy and crisis management. According to this lens, a dyslexic person who finds reading texts in 'standard' formats hard because of dyslexia may also *because of dyslexia* have excellent people skills.[32] It is worth asking students what they feel about this theory of 'spiky profiles', and whether they feel it accurately describes them. As Ambereen Dadabhoy and Nedda Mehdizadeh write, educators can have a number of concerns when adjusting

---

[31] Jenara Nerenberg, *Divergent Mind* (London: HarperOne, 2020), 167.

[32] Stanislas Dehaene traces an evolutionary advantage in dyslexia, explaining that the very brain processes that make mirror-image letters (p, q, d, b) difficult for dyslexic people to distinguish also conferred a quick-thinking ability useful for survival as it enables a person to respond quickly to a threat without wasting time distinguishing between their left or right hand side as the source of the threat, *Reading in the Brain: The New Science of How We Read* (London: Penguin Viking, 2009), 305. Helen Taylor and Martin David Vestergaard discuss the purpose of dyslexic cognition—what it is evolutionarily *for*; 'Developmental Dyslexia: Disorder of Specialization in Exploration', *Frontiers in Psychology* (2022).

classrooms to suit their students' needs and positionalities; I address this issue with relation to neurodivergence in the next subsection.[33]

Adjustments Educators Can Make as Part of Business as Usual

Why don't we take neurodivergence as our norm, and then adjust our classes, on a case-by-case basis, for neurotypical people? This imagined inversion of the usual status quo can keep us conscious of the way in which even having to ask for adjustments can leave students feeling marginalised and ashamed. By contrast, adjustments that are made compassionately, completely, quickly, and consistently, can feel euphoric for neurodivergent people. Educators should not engage in arguments with students about the adjustments they request. Rather than humiliating and invalidating students in this way, what if we simply trust them when they tell us what they need and act accordingly. Making adjustments for neurodivergent students does not disadvantage neurotypical students: these students are not in opposition to each other. Making classrooms comfortable for neurodivergent people helps to make them joyful, inclusive, comradely places: an atmosphere that benefits everyone.

As well as asking students about their individual needs, below are some adjustments educators can make. Reading this list, educators may experience a number of concerns, which include:

- What if my students have competing needs? For example, what if one student stims by drumming on the table and another needs silence in order to focus? Such questions can be reframed so that, instead of pitting neurodivergent people's needs against each other, educators ask, 'how can I best accommodate both students at once?' Solutions come from multiple angles, from the practical (giving the first student a soft cushion to drum on and affirming to the other student that they are welcome to wear headphones and sit in the quieter area of the room) to the interpersonal: trusting that students can draw on their relationships with each other inside and outside the classroom to find a way to learn together

[33] Ambereen Dadabhoy and Nedda Mehdizadeh, *Anti-Racist Shakespeare* (Cambridge: Cambridge University Press, 2024), 57–59.

without the educator necessarily having to mediate between students' different needs.

- What if I make a mistake, use the wrong terminology or forget to make a particular student's adjustments? Apologise, rectify the situation as soon as possible, and move on. Do something to care for yourself afterwards.
- What if students take advantage of my questions about their needs to ask for things that would simply disrupt the class, or challenge my authority? I invite educators to consider what status quo is being disrupted here and whether that status quo is enforcing ableist ideas about learning. For example, might it be an advantage to relax a rule about no student leaving the room during class, so that some students can calm and focus their thoughts in a quiet room if they need to? Set and keep boundaries about those adjustments, clearly explaining what you can and can't offer, and why.

The below list of adjustments educators can make is not exhaustive and I invite readers to edit and add to it. Some educators' power to make adjustments is more limited than others'. An adjunct on a zero-hours contract entering a classroom with blinking fluorescent lights, loud whirring air con or projectors, and no captioning software may know that these features of the room prevent their autistic students from learning well. But, they may feel too exhausted, poorly connected in the university they are working at short-term, and poorly paid to do anything about it. I have made this list long partly so that any educator should be able to find some things that they *can* do; that thing might be sending one email asking how to get a better teaching room.

- Make your classroom relaxed: explicitly encourage students to move in and out of the room as they like, wear headphones, stim and tic whenever they want.[34] Offer items to fidget with (stress balls, pipe cleaners, string),

---

[34] Stimming: Words, sounds, and/or movements (often repetitive) that delight, situate, and engage the self. Stimming is often strongly associated with autism, but many neurodivergent people stim. Waggling hands up and down is an example of stimming; pacing, moving the body into and out of certain positions, drumming fingers, and making sounds with one's mouth can also be stimming. Practically anything can become a stim – neurodivergent people are extremely creative. Tics

put elastic exercise bands on chair legs for students to bounce their legs against. Take agreed breaks at various points.

- Book a 'quiet room' nearby where students can decompress (a 'vacant/engaged' sign made from a piece of paper stops somebody bursting in on somebody else).
- Offer a traffic light system of stickers, which people can stick on their clothes or laptop, to aid communication in class: green sticker means 'feel free to approach me and chat'; amber means 'don't approach me first, let me approach you'; red means 'I'm just here to listen, not chat'. Prepare for many students to select red by considering how you will feel comfortable with students' silence. What stereotypes do you have in your mind about silent students (that they aren't engaged, perhaps? That they're thinking hard? That they dislike the class, or don't understand it?) and interrogate where those stereotypes and assumptions come from. Saying calmly, 'it's alright, we can sit in silence' can sometimes be enough.
- Offer simple written and verbal summaries of key ideas in classes, set reading, and lectures. If you can, take Easy Read training and draw on Easy Read image banks, to make these summaries more effective. Easy Read is a way of presenting information in a clear, accessible format, designed specifically for people with learning disabilities.
- Provide visual summaries of key ideas and set reading.
- Stream/record teaching and provide transcripts. Additionally, ask students who attended to blog about the class, so others can participate without having to leave home if to do so is overwhelming or inaccessible. The blog can be an assignment that helps students develop writing skills and draw inspiration from the many other Shakespeare blogs online.
- On slides and handouts, use sans-serif fonts and create a high contrast between the text and the background (for instance dark black text against

are involuntary words, sounds, or movements, they can be associated not only with conditions like Tourette's syndrome but also with for instance episodes of stress. An eye spasm can be a tic, and so can vocalising particular words in the middle of a sentence. For an illuminating description of tics, see Tourette's Hero (Jess Thom)'s website: touretteshero.com/safe/category/blog/tics [accessed March 2023].

a lime green background). Don't put more than a few lines of text on a single slide or section of a handout. Read this text aloud for students.

- Provide pieces of paper and pens and/or keyboards on the table for students who communicate best in writing.
- Include asynchronous elements, like online discussion boards, to accommodate difference paces of engagement with the class material.
- Disseminate photographs (with written descriptions) of the space where the class will happen, the route to the class, and key people involved.
- Offer a buddy scheme where people who are anxious about attending class will get a buddy who might help in various mutually agreed ways, for example walking to the class with them, checking in with them at various points.
- Use content warnings for students for subjects that can cause distress including sexual violence, violence, racism, homophobia, transphobia, and ableism.
- Demonstrate practical activities, and how to navigate resources, step by step before the students complete the activity or use the resource themselves. For instance, if you suggest that students use a database like DEEP or the Folger First Folio online, demonstrate using it step by step in class.[35]
- Provide as much information as you can (e.g. handouts, slides) in advance.
- Caption videos; make sure speakers use a microphone.
- At the start of a class or course of study, ask students to tell each other their preferred communication styles so that they can adapt to each other (e.g. 'I prefer verbal communication to written communication; unbroken blocks of text aren't accessible to me'). This can help you to prepare ahead when it comes to accommodating potentially 'competing' needs (like the need for drumming and the need for silence used as an example elsewhere in this section).
- Ask students how they find the lighting and temperature and adjust if necessary.

---

[35] DEEP: Database of Early English Playbooks http://deep.sas.upenn.edu/ [accessed August 2022].

- Start a lecture or class by describing yourself (for people who are blind or have visual processing differences) and invite others to do the same. For example I normally say 'I am a white woman in her late 30s, with brown hair in a skin fade, wearing a [insert colour] top'.
- Interrogate assumptions about intelligence (e.g. that spontaneous dialogue, remembering large chunks of text, and fluent reading of Shakespearean verse equal intelligence, whereas silence means a student is not engaged) and avoid basing students' grades or evaluations on these assumptions. As work by disability-studies scholars like Margaret Price, CF Goodey, and Jay Dolmage shows, the project of measuring human 'intelligence' has frequently been used to dehumanise disabled people, with definitions of intelligence shifting over time. Educators do not need to judge how intelligent their students are, but to facilitate their learning and engagement with course material.
- Embrace the fact that students have different working and reading speeds. Rather than stipulating that a certain task 'should' take a certain amount of time, work out whether students need you to accommodate their working speeds better, or help them to work out how much they can get done in a particular time (I discuss this further in Section 2).
- Say 'welcome' to a student who comes in late.
- Fix 'access clashes' (where one student's access needs seem to clash with another's) in a compassionate way that avoids asking students to mask. For example, if a student needs to rap on the table to stim but it distracts another student, do not insist anyone stops stimming or magically controls their distraction levels. Instead try giving the stimming student a mouse pad or something soft to rap on that muffles the noise, and enable students to sit where they like so those who are distracted by the rapping can sit out of eye and earshot of it.
- Ask students what they need, accepting that their needs may change.

When educators make as many of these basic adjustments as they can from the beginning, students will not have to bring them up themselves, and can instead use any group discussion to go into more detail about their individual needs. When making adjustments, do not make a fanfare about it or expect gratitude: adjustments should be a basic part of your job. Ellingson writes, 'When I do secure a disability accommodation, the cost is an implicit requirement that I be demonstrably appreciative of my university's generosity, performing a relentless, cheerful gratitude and remaining polite, patient and nonconfrontational in the face of ableist policies, practices, and microaggressions on my campus'.[36] This issue may already have come up in classroom discussion: one potential reading of the scene from *King Lear* with which I opened this section is that Edgar is deliberately exaggerating his role of Gloucester's saviour and helper, disempowering Gloucester in the process. After listing their adjustments, some students might end with a joke like ' . . . and I'll have a Frappuccino too!' or 'will you come and clean my room while you're at it?'. Students are taught that adjustments are a luxury, like a posh iced coffee, and that they blur the boundaries between what is and isn't core to an educator's job. Adjustments are central to our jobs; we should be clear about what we can and cannot offer. This includes acknowledging what we cannot change by ourselves. For example offering students choice of formats for classwork and assessments (e.g. poster, essay, presentation, performance, podcast) is helpful for neurodiverse classrooms because it enables students to demonstrate how they fulfil learning objectives in the way most accessible to them. For instance, Varsha Panjwani has explained the ability of Shakespeare podcasting to enable diverse voices to be heard in Shakespeare studies; this includes neurodivergent voices.[37] Barbara Pavey, Margaret Meehan and Alan Waugh suggest that for dyslexic students, educators add to the usual unseen examination a choice of: 'i) an examination with a "seen" paper, ii) a set of short questions, iii) a portfolio, iv) a presentation, v) a poster', noting, 'an innovative practitioner who was willing to give students a choice of even two or three of these may find, through providing this equality of opportunity, that there are benefits in terms of student application, commitment,

---

[36] Ellingson, 'A Leg to Stand on', 18.

[37] Varsha Panjwani, *Podcasting and Feminist Shakespeare Pedagogy* (Cambridge: Cambridge University Press, 2023).

confidence, and outcomes'.[38] However, many educators are not in a position to effect these changes single-handedly, or quickly enough to benefit the students currently in their classes. It will take a collective change for education to become truly accessible to neurodivergent people.

Adjustments as a Source of Literary Analysis

When we make access the foundation of our teaching, adjustments for neurodivergent students can be a rich source of new literary analyses and discoveries. I end this section with an example of this, inspired by the acting coach Petronilla Whitfield's Shakespeare class designs for dyslexic actors. Educators might provide plenty of images and less text in their slides, handouts, and other class materials to make class more accessible to dyslexic students. Though this accessibility groundwork is vital, Whitfield's work suggests that we can go further: by centring dyslexic ways of learning, we can generatively de-centre students' rigid text-based relationships to Shakespeare. Focusing exclusively on Shakespeare's written language can occlude students' appreciation of its embodied and visual aspects. Centring instead visual imagery and the body can empower dyslexic students to draw on their strengths and enable both dyslexic and non-dyslexic students to understand Shakespeare's use of visuality and kinesis more profoundly. Whitfield demonstrates that neurodivergent ways of thinking can be a fount of new perspectives, insights, and ideas about Shakespeare. When educators enable neurodivergent students, these students are encouraged to develop in their *own* neurodivergent way rather than following neurotypical bench-marks. Whitfield describes exercises designed to foster spontaneous inter-action among her ensemble, which included a dyslexic student, David.[39] Whitfield applies research that shows that dyslexic people can be especially good at synthesising their brains' visual and kinaesthetic capacities.[40] In

[38] Barbara Pavey, Margaret Meehan, and Alan Waugh, *Dyslexia-Friendly Further and Higher Education* (London: SAGE, 2009), 21.

[39] Petronilla Whitfield, *Teaching Strategies for Neurodiversity and Dyslexia in Actor Training: Sensing Shakespeare* (London: Routledge, 2020), 21.

[40] Whitfield, *Teaching Strategies for Neurodiversity and Dyslexia in Actor Training*, 31–32.

order to give dyslexic students the opportunity to draw on these strengths, she based her classroom exercises around drawings and movement, asking students to create storyboards, list moments of physical movement in Shakespeare, draw a character's lines as pictures, analyse drawings and photos, and express and interpret texts' meanings through movement. Moreover, though reading aloud will benefit many students' learning (and for this reason it is a useful classroom tool), Whitfield states that there is no need to require every student to do so because this relies on a false equation of fluent reading-aloud with understanding; a student who reads a text aloud fluently may well have misinterpreted some of its vocabulary and context.[41] As she notes, asking a dyslexic student to read an unseen text aloud fluently can be inaccessible and shaming to them, precipitating life-long damage to their self-esteem and making it hard for them to enjoy or benefit from studying Shakespeare. These exercises can help to engage and stimulate students, Whitfield argues, pointing out that as much as we fête Shakespeare as a wordsmith, sometimes his text does not 'excite' students or actors' imaginations in the ways that imagery and physical movement can.[42] For instance, in one exercise, she read the text aloud herself and then asked students to speak each sentence aloud; 'As they spoke the text, each student used physical actions to express the core of meaning or feeling, as they saw it'.[43] This, she writes, removed the stressful load of reading written text from David, affording him 'more freedom to exercise his acting instincts'.[44]

Educators can use similar classroom exercises, asking students to draw or model clay in response to a passage the educator, or another student, reads aloud, then asking them to reflect on how they found the exercise and how de-centring the text enables them to see Shakespeare's language. Offering a range of art materials (charcoal, paints, pencils, modelling clay, pipe cleaners, paper, and string for weaving and tying) enables students to choose what they like and avoids offering a single option that is accessible only to some students (for instance, dyspraxic students may

[41] Whitfield, *Teaching Strategies for Neurodiversity and Dyslexia in Actor Training*, 204.

[42] Whitfield, *Teaching Strategies for Neurodiversity and Dyslexia in Actor Training*, 33.

[43] Whitfield, *Teaching Strategies for Neurodiversity and Dyslexia in Actor Training*, 22.

[44] Whitfield, *Teaching Strategies for Neurodiversity and Dyslexia in Actor Training*, 22.

find it unhelpful to be asked to engage in complex movements or manipulations of materials). It is crucial to emphasise to students that they are not being evaluated on the quality of their artworks; this is not an art class: rather, they are pursuing this exercise to discover how it might be useful to them in understanding Shakespeare.

I have found the Soothsayer's prophecy in *Cymbeline* particularly effective for encouraging students not only to engage with Shakespeare's words in different ways (movement, drawing, analysis of the language), but for analysing the different kinds of knowledge that they derive from these varying approaches. The Soothsayer interprets this prophecy purely in linguistic terms, stating for instance that 'tender air' is 'mollis aer' in Latin, which sounds like 'mulier' (woman). However, precisely because he is a soothsayer who deals in obscure and occult arts, his prophecy and its interpretation are hard to follow on a purely linguistic level. His prophecy runs:

> Whenas a lion's whelp shall, to himself unknown, without seeking find, and be embraced by a piece of tender air; and when from a stately cedar shall be lopped branches, which, being dead many years, shall after revive, be jointed to the old stock, and freshly grow; then shall Posthumus end his miseries, Britain be fortunate and flourish in peace and plenty.[45]

He interprets:

> Thou, Leonatus, art the lion's whelp;
> The fit and apt construction of thy name,
> Being *leo-natus*, doth import so much.
> [*To Cymbeline*] The piece of tender air, thy virtuous daughter,
> Which we call *mollis aer*, and *mollis aer*
> We term it *mulier*; [*To Posthumus*] which *mulier* I divine

---

45　William Shakespeare, *Cymbeline*, ed. Martin Butler (Cambridge: Cambridge University Press, 2004), V.v.435–40.

> Is thy most constant wife; who, even now,
> Answering the letter of the oracle,
> Unknown to you, unsought, were clipp'd about
> With this most tender air (*Cymbeline*, V.v.440–450)

The prophecy is a single sentence with many clauses, describing some odd visuals – what is a 'piece' of air, for example? Linguistic difficulties students might experience can be tackled by inviting them to picture or otherwise sense the prophecy and thereby bring out the tactile and kinetic dimension to the soothsayer's words. Mulier = mollis aer might be felt as both a sensory and linguistic pun, for example, likening a wife's soft embraces to the feel of air. The Soothsayer completely forgets about the branch in his interpretation, but the image of the branches being chopped from the cedar, lying dead, being grafted back on to the cedar and beginning to grow again offers interesting kinetic possibilities. Students might draw the prophecy's imagery, move in response to the life-cycle of the branches, or assemble items that interpret the text (a puff of air, a branch). They might use gesture and drawing to interpret the shifts between the text of the prophecy and the way the soothsayer interprets them: what is the difference between being 'embraced' and being 'clipped about' for example?

The Soothsayer probably makes his words foggy and hard to understand immediately so that he can be the one to interpret them; his privileged position in Cymbeline's court, and in the play, derives from his relationship to 'the letter of the oracle'. This resembles one way of approaching Shakespeare's works: as hard-to-decipher texts, which need a privileged class of people – literary critics who are skilled at interpreting written language – to interpret them. This approach to Shakespeare leaves everyone who is not in that privileged class – that is most people, and among them many dyslexic students – unenthused and excluded from the centre of literary activity. Reclaiming the ability to interpret the Soothsayer's prophecy in an embodied and sensory way not only genuinely helps us to make sense of what he is saying, but also usefully decentres that elitist version of Shakespearean criticism. In his prophecy and his interpretation of it, the Soothsayer resembles an unhelpful version of Shakespeare and the literary critics who interpret him: Shakespeare as a dispenser of abstruse language which only certain people are qualified to engage with and explain.

As you can see, exercises like this, which are essentially motivated by adjusting for dyslexic students, are not about giving dyslexic students an 'easier' experience of Shakespeare which veils his complexity. Rather, by centring what we might think of as dyslexic learning styles, we get to the centre of much of what Shakespeare is about – embodiment and intriguing imagery – and get behind his tricky-to-read language. Educators can integrate these drawing/movement exercises into analyses of rhythm, imagery, and structure. We can relate the exercises to ideas about embodied cognition in the theatre; for example, Evelyn Tribble explores how early modern actors would have used bodily gestures to help them learn their lines, and reduced the load on their brains by not attempting to 'know' the entirety of the play and instead trusting to other actors and to playhouse documents like plots to embody the knowledge about the play in a shared way.[46] Educators might adapt these exercises in conversation with Shakespeare scholarship in a variety of ways. Via the work of scholars like Simon Smith, educators might centre discussions around the use of onstage music, incorporating musical performances into classes.[47] Or, educators might draw on Harry McCarthy's research with actors on physical gameplay in early modern drama. Discussing John Marston and John Day, McCarthy argues that it is usually not enough to read early modern plays about games; it is crucial to physically play the games in order to appreciate their impact on plot, character, emotion, and language: 'game and dialogue (and, therefore plot) unfold simultaneously', their temporalities affecting each other.[48] At one point, he noted, the audience in the Sam Wanamaker Theatre actually seemed to enjoy, and train their attention on, the shuttlecock game in Marston's *What You Will*, rather than the dialogue:

[46] Evelyn Tribble, *Cognition in the Globe: Attention and Memory in Shakespeare's Theatre* (New York: Palgrave, 2011).

[47] Simon Smith, *Musical Response in the Early Modern Playhouse 1603–1625* (Cambridge: Cambridge University Press, 2017).

[48] Harry McCarthy, *Boy Actors in Early Modern England* (Cambridge: Cambridge University Press, 2022), 114, 117–18, and chapter 3, passim.

a clear sign of the ways in which physicality, movement, and visuality can supersede the mere text of an early modern play.[49]

Educators might consider how incorporating discussion of these critics' works into their classes can open out into considerations of neurodivergence. For example, Tribble examines how the early modern practice of acting in parts (where each actor only learnt their individual part and cues, rather than trying to memorise the whole play) reduced actors' cognitive load. Students might consider neurodiversity in this context: what might cognitive load look like for a neurodivergent actor? Asking the question, 'what if Shakespeare wrote for neurodivergent actors?' can help neurodivergent students to see people like them as *already there* in Shakespearean texts and playhouse practices.

As Whitfield notes, not all dyslexic people will benefit from, or like, exercises like storyboarding or the drawing exercise described above.[50] One reason for this could be that a dyslexic student has other conditions affecting their mobility or ability to process spoken words. Or, drawing and storyboarding might simply not be their thing. Though Whitfield's exercise emphasises dyslexic strengths, in her study of adult dyslexia, Kelli Sandman-Hurley found that several dyslexic adults she interviewed felt that emphasis on dyslexic strengths or dyslexia as a 'gift' elides the real struggle of being dyslexic in an ableist education system.[51] Moreover, dyslexic students may desire to linger over written language; one of Sandman-Hurley's dyslexic interviewees, Chuck, states,

> When you can't help but take your time, you have time to notice a lot. There is room for those most elementary and forceful words to linger, for connections across texts to fall in place, and for pertinent questions to emerge and demand attention. When you have to labour to string words in the

[49] McCarthy, *Boy Actors*, 128.

[50] Whitfield, *Teaching Strategies for Neurodiversity and Dyslexia in Actor Training*, 150–61.

[51] Kelli Sandman-Hurley, *The Adult Side of Dyslexia* (London: Jessica Kingsley, 2021), 89–90.

> right order, you cannot help but dwell upon and participate
> in the author's own sentence construction.[52]

The exercises I described in this section are *an* option for the class, not 'the dyslexic option'. These exercises are about recognising the specific strengths that a particular neurodivergent condition might bring to our understanding of Shakespeare, and allowing these strengths to inform the class's learning as a community, across neurotypes.

Classrooms can be high stakes environments, for reasons ranging from students linking their 'success' in class to their career-goals and later educational goals, to the dynamics of the classroom as a 'public' social space. A student's sense of safety and confidence might, because of experiences in past classrooms, feel fragile and vulnerable as 'gossamer, feathers, air'. Shaming neurodivergent students in our classrooms can hurt them for the rest of their lives.[53] Shaming educators may seem like the terrifying monster Edgar describes teaching Gloucester his lesson at the top of the cliff,

> methought his eyes
> Were two full moons; he had a thousand noses,
> Horns whelked and waved like the enragèd sea.
> It was some fiend. (*King Lear*, IV.vi.69–71)

Classrooms can seem a cliff edge for some, even when the ground seems flat to others.

When Polonius asks Hamlet what he is reading, Hamlet responds 'words, words, words'.[54] This can be read as a neurodivergent answer in varying ways: an autistic Hamlet, interpreting the question in a literal way, might helpfully respond 'words, words, words'; a dyslexic Hamlet, battling

---

[52] Sandman-Hurley, *The Adult Side of Dyslexia*, 29.

[53] Sandman-Hurley documents some of the effects of this shaming, *The Adult Side of Dyslexia*, 27.

[54] William Shakespeare, *Hamlet, Prince of Denmark*, ed. Heather Hirschfeld (Cambridge: Cambridge University Press, 2019), II.ii.189.

through an inaccessible text, might respond in the same way. Polonius again attempts to probe into the specifics of what Hamlet is reading and asks 'what's the matter?' Hamlet asks 'between who?' (II.ii.190–1); again, this response is legibly autistic and dyslexic: Hamlet might be taking Polonius' question literally, and/or cleverly deflecting Polonius away from close analysis of a text he cannot read while another person is putting him under pressure. In this section, I have argued that Shakespeare does not have to be merely written 'words, words, words'. While there is room in every lesson for close analysis of Shakespeare's language, we can conduct close reading in generatively accessible ways. There are plenty of ways to do this beyond the exercises I focused on in this section; I might have talked, for example, about creative exercises based on asynchronous discussions that can aid autistic students. Accessibility means making space for all students to learn together, not setting neurodivergent students where neurotypicals stand.

2 No Single Way to Read Shakespeare

Clear Summary

- Often educational institutions assume that the 'right' way to read and interpret Shakespeare is the neurotypical way.
- Neurodivergent ways of reading and interpreting Shakespeare can result in new insights.
- We should encourage neurodivergent readings and interpretations of Shakespeare in our classroom.
- One example of encouraging neurodivergent ways of reading and interpreting Shakespeare is exploring ways of engaging with Shakespeare with different levels of focus, and according to different timescales.

Francis, When Thou Wilt: Shakespeare on Crip Time

In *1 Henry IV*, Prince Hal and his accomplice Poins make life difficult for Francis the drawer (waiter) in the tavern they are drinking at. Hal and Poins hatch a plot to position themselves at two different locations – Hal onstage, and Poins offstage – and each demand Francis's attention. As Poins calls Francis insistently, Hal keeps Francis talking to prevent him attending to Poins; moreover, Hal frequently changes the topics in his dialogue with Francis. As Hal accurately predicts, as a result, Francis finds it difficult to concentrate or complete his job tasks (serving Hal and Poins, attending to guests). These difficulties are exacerbated because Francis is paid to be polite and helpful to customers, rather taken with Hal, and conscious of the power Hal and Poins have over him (not least because Hal is heir to the throne). Torn between Hal and Poins, Francis wrestles with distraction:

POINS :   [*WITHIN*] Francis! *Enter* [*FRANCIS, a*] *Drawer*

FRANCIS: Anon, anon, sir. Look down into the Pomgarnet, Ralph!

PRINCE: Come hither, Francis.

FRANCIS: My lord?

PRINCE: How long hast thou to serve, Francis?

FRANCIS: Forsooth, five years, and as much as to—

POINS: [*WITHIN*] Francis!

FRANCIS: Anon, anon, sir.

PRINCE: Five year! By'r lady, a long lease for the clinking of pewter. But, Francis, darest thou be so valiant as to play the coward with thy indenture and show it a fair pair of heels and run from it?

FRANCIS: O Lord, sir, I'll be sworn upon all the books in England, I could find in my heart—

POINS: [*WITHIN*] Francis!

FRANCIS: Anon, sir.

PRINCE: How old art thou, Francis?

FRANCIS: Let me see: about Michaelmas next I shall be—

POINS: [*WITHIN*] Francis!

FRANCIS: Anon, sir – pray stay a little, my lord.

PRINCE: Nay but hark you, Francis: for the sugar thou gavest me,'twas a pennyworth, was't not?

FRANCIS: O Lord, I would it had been two!

PRINCE: I will give thee for it a thousand pound. Ask me when thou wilt, and thou shalt have it.

POINS: [*WITHIN*] Francis!

FRANCIS: Anon, anon.

PRINCE: Anon, Francis? No, Francis; but to-morrow, Francis. Or, Francis, a-Thursday. Or indeed Francis, when thou wilt. But Francis!

FRANCIS: My lord?

PRINCE: Wilt thou rob this leathern-jerkin, crystal-button, not-pated, agate-ring, puke-stocking, caddis-garter, smooth-tongue, Spanish-pouch?

FRANCIS: O Lord, sir, who do you mean?

PRINCE: Why then your brown bastard is your only drink. For look you, Francis, your white canvas doublet will sully. In Barbary, sir, it cannot come to so much.

FRANCIS: What, sir?

POINS: [*WITHIN*] Francis!

PRINCE: Away, you rogue, dost thou not hear them call?

Here they both call him; the Drawer stands amazed, not knowing which way to go (II.iv.30–69)

Hal exerts his power over the conversation, to Francis's detriment. Hal switches topics (from Francis's job circumstances, to Francis's age, to the cost of sugar, to a list of adjectives describing Francis's master, to different drinks), introducing new questions whilst Francis is still replying to an earlier question; Poins' calls further disrupt Francis's attempts to talk with Hal. Poignantly, Francis attempts to connect with Hal, endeavouring to respond to Hal's questions properly and to follow through on his affectionate gift of sugar ('would it had been two!'). However, Francis quickly loses his handle on the conversation.

Hal inappositely calls *Francis* the 'rogue' in the situation, then Francis's master the Vintner enters and tells Francis off: 'What, standest thou still and hearest such a calling? Look to the guests within' (II.iv.70–1). At this point, neither Hal nor Poins stands up for Francis, despite having been the ones to get him in trouble. Hal's boast that he is 'sworn brother to a leash of drawers' (II.iv.6) is self-glorifying; he seems to value Francis only insofar as he can tease him. It looks to the Vintner like Francis is not working hard. However, Shakespeare shows us what Francis had to contend with: the distractions and obstacles that left him at a standstill. In the classroom, students may appear confused and unable to focus; educators may blame the student for not working hard and not meeting the learning milestones and deadlines they (the educators) had stipulated. The student may find it difficult in the moment to explain, and/or lack supporters who can help them to explain, what they were contending with. Compassionate educators seek to uncover and empathise with the distractions and obstacles students face as they engage in classwork and homework.

Shakespeare makes highly visible the clash between Francis's rhythm of thought, speech, and understanding and Hal's quick-fire attempts to undermine Francis. We might productively relate this scene to our own mode of engaging with the play. As audience members and readers, we may find ourselves more attuned to Francis's temporality and feel as distracted and bewildered as he is; we may more naturally follow Hal's rapid questioning, or Poins' intermittent repetitions; we may feel out of sync with all of the characters. This scene gives us an opportunity to see distraction and mind-wandering as key to Shakespearean writing: something stimulating, something to dwell on. Francis gets distracted, but Shakespeare does not position the problem so much within Francis as within Hal's deliberate failure to accommodate Francis's thinking and communication style. Hal takes advantage of Francis, stymying him for fun rather than letting him in to the conversation and giving him access to understanding and the ability to set the conversational agenda. Francis's 'what sir?' is the most sensible line in the whole exchange.

For many neurodivergent students, the experience of wading through conversations that are dominated by others' conversational norms and then being blamed for becoming distracted, having too many or too few topics in their minds, answering too quickly or too slowly, is all too familiar. Students with ADHD are one example, as are (this is not an exhaustive list) students under stress, tired and fatigued students, students taking medication that affects their memory, mood, and attention, students with memory differences (for instance due to dementia), and autistic students attempting to focus on the class topic(s) but finding synchronous conversation hard or distracted by hypersensitivity to noise. Even worse is when neurotypical people drive home the shame of this by suggesting that neurodivergent students inherently cannot understand the class material, or aren't working hard or fast enough. Instead, as I discussed in Section 1, as educators we should compassionately ask our students what they need and adjust our behaviour accordingly.

One stereotype about great art is that it is created through intense focus and that it can only be appreciated and understood through intense focus on the part of academics and students. What if we acknowledge that this is a myth which best serves one subset of humanity: people who tend to hyperfocus on just one thing, and whose object of focus is valued by society? What if we celebrate the artistic creation that occurs in bitty, stop-and-start ways, that does not reach milestones or completion when it is 'supposed to'? What if we appreciate the art in conversation and thought that shoots in many directions like fireworks, involves dynamic interruptions to introduce new ideas and connections between ideas? What if, without them being in competition, intense focus and mind-wandering, as well as all possible versions of human attention and timekeeping, were valued, peacefully coexisting, approaches to literature?

Shakespeare frequently makes divergent modes of reading and thinking central to plot and character. Malvolio reads the letters MOAI in a supposed love-letter from Olivia, and transposes them to make them say 'Malvolio', thus propelling his ill-fated seduction-attempt. Fundamental to the plot of *Romeo and Juliet* is the Servant's inability to read Old Capulet's guest list for his ball. The Servant asks Romeo to read the list for him in Act 1; in so doing, he lets Romeo know about the details of the ball, precipitating Romeo's meeting with Juliet. The Servant may do this unwittingly, or perhaps he chooses Romeo to read for him because he wants to cause mischief by giving a Montague insider information on Capulet affairs. Neurodivergent ways of reading (and resistance to reading) and interpretation, then, had aesthetic value for Shakespeare. I have argued elsewhere that reading *King John* autistically enables us to revel in the play's repetitions as a source of politicised joy.[55] One common classroom exercise is to have

---

[55] Laura Seymour, 'Shakespearean Echolalia: Autism and Versification in *King John*', *Shakespeare* 18(3) (2022), 335–51.

students walk around the classroom repeating single lines and repeating their lines in different ways, tones, and speeds when they encounter each other, to test out what kinds of new feelings and relationships spring from such encounters. Such an exercise is practically built in to any performance of the highly repetitive Scene 3.1 in *King John*: we do not have to change Shakespeare's script very much, or at all, to perform this exercise. Julia Miele Rodas argues that the rhythms of autistic repetition are poetic and only ableism prevents us seeing this; Ronald Schleifer contends that the 'primal cry' and melodies of Tourette syndrome share in what is at the heart of poetry.[56] Neurodivergent people can both read *with* and perform *with* neurodivergence. Describing a 2010 performance of *A Midsummer Night's Dream* with homeless and disabled actors in Paris, Isabelle Schwartz-Gastine discusses how the actor playing Starveling had an ebullient personality, a constant tremor in his hand, and could not read or write, which respectively helped him convey Starveling's lionish exuberance, nervousness, and 'slow[ness] of study'.[57] Classes could watch and discuss videos of neurodivergent actors discussing their process, such as those involved in Australian organisation SpectrumSpace's *A Midsummer Night's Dream*.[58] Neurodivergence offers us generative ways to read and perform: new melodies, temporalities, ideas, and modes of engagement with Shakespeare.

Several students in our classes will be reading Shakespeare on *crip time*. Crip time means the different temporalities of disabled existence.[59] In the context of neurodivergence, crip time can include schedule-clashes between classes and medical/psychiatric appointments, the speed at which students naturally work best (which may not coincide with institutional deadlines),

---

[56] Julia Miele Rodas, *Autistic Disturbances* (Ann Arbor, MI: Michigan University Press, 2018), 7, 44; Ronald Schleifer, 'The Poetics of Tourettes Syndrome', *New Literary History* 32(3) (2001), 563–84.

[57] Isabelle Schwartz-Gastine, 'Performing *a Midsummer Night's Dream* with the Homeless (and Others) in Paris', *Borrowers and Lenders* 8(2) (2013), (pp. 1–14), 9.

[58] 'Reimagined Dream: A Neurodiverse Retelling' shakespearereloaded.edu.au/events/reimagined-dream-neurodiverse-retelling [accessed 13 June 2024].

[59] Cf. e.g. Ellen Samuels, 'Six Ways of Looking at Crip Time', in Alice Wong, ed., *Disability Visibility* (London: Vintage, 2020), 189–96.

fatigue or chemo brain rendering students unable to arrive at class 'on time', students with anxiety hovering outside classes preparing themselves to enter, students with depression leaving school or university before their course ends, hyperfocus and special interests motivating students to read and work for hours, the different times students take to process information and formulate their ideas in written and verbal form, the varying times students require to transition between tasks, the times in their lives that students come to education because of their individual needs and/or (usually and) the ways society hinders them from entering education. As I have argued elsewhere, crip time is 'kairotic in its own way'.[60] Rather than moving to the swift beat of neurotypical dialogue, autistic people, for example, may repeat words, emotions, and questions and answers from minutes, hours, and months previously, thus bringing issues to our attention that others thought were done with.

In *1 Henry IV*, characters' communication styles are profoundly linked to plot and character. Hal distracts Francis and talks as if he himself is distracted. The scene between Hal and Francis is symptomatic of Hal's meandering life-trajectory throughout the play, which attracts comments from other characters about whether Hal has forgotten his supposed life-goal of being a good monarch, is moving towards this goal too slowly, and is deliberately distracting himself from the court by spending time in taverns. Deriving from *dis-trahere* (Latin: to draw away), 'distraction' suggests movement away from normative routes. 'Distraction', in Shakespeare's time, could also mean 'madness'; there is substantial overlap between Hal's distracting nature (both in the sense of being attractive to others, and interrupting others' attention), and his role as 'madcap' (*1 Henry IV*, I.ii.116; IV.i.95). Hal's structural power means that his distracting japes are unlikely to rebound as harmfully on himself as they might on Francis. Several factors disempower Francis and make it hard for him to assert his needs, not least the fact that Francis is an 'indentured' worker whereas Hal is about to become the ruler of the country Francis lives in. Francis's refrain 'Anon, anon, sir' encapsulates his constant stressful struggle to conform to temporal norms imposed on him by those socially above him (the sirs of his world).[61]

---

[60] Seymour, 'Shakespearean Echolalia', 338.

[61] In many British schools, and perhaps elsewhere, male teachers still require their students to call them 'Sir'.

Neurodivergent students may see aspects of their own experience in Francis'. Instead of leaving students feeling like they have no choice but to say 'Anon, anon' to neurotypical norms of reading and studying Shakespeare, what if, attentive to power structures at play in the classroom, we read Shakespeare on crip time, saw life in Francis's way, took things at Francis's pace? What if we said, 'Francis, when thou wilt'?

Reading with a 'Wandering Mind'

The notion that we are 'supposed' to read Shakespeare in any particular way very often is informed by neuro-ableism. Freeing ourself from this notion enhances our literary-critical abilities. I focus here on one example: reading with distraction and mind-wandering. The normative idea that we should read or watch Shakespeare in a laser-focused way and stay 'on-topic' limits students whose minds naturally connect many topics at once, and who find long periods of single focus exhausting and unhelpful for thinking. All too often, the person defining what counts as a relevant topic, and as staying 'on' this topic, is not the neurodivergent student themselves. Rather, these students grapple with ableist educational norms that are alien to them. We should not assume that Shakespeare himself even wanted his audiences and readers only to engage with his work in a single-focused way. In her Element *This Distracted Globe*, Jennifer Edwards draws on show reports at the Globe to illuminate how distractions from the surrounding area (from pigeons flying past to pieces of set coming loose) form part of present-day Shakespeare performances for actors, front of house staff, and audiences.[62] In 'Shakespeare and the Wandering Mind', Raphael Lyne argues that Shakespeare was alert to the creative potential of mind-wandering and as such explicitly invites audiences to become distracted, and even bored, integrating their own thoughts with what happens in his plays. Lyne discusses mind-wandering both as a theme of Shakespearean drama and a way of reading: 'Shakespeare draws out the things our minds do when they wander'.[63] For Lyne,

[62] Jennifer Edwards, *This Distracted Globe* (Cambridge: Cambridge University Press, 2023).

[63] Raphael Lyne, 'Shakespeare and the Wandering Mind', *Journal of the British Academy* 8 (2020) (pp. 1–27), 2.

acknowledging that human minds frequently need to wander to think well enables us to notice that Shakespeare's characters' minds often visibly wander, 'there are inevitably moments when onstage minds seem to be busy elsewhere, not focused on what we can see and hear. Such moments are illuminated by emerging thinking in cognitive science that suggests human minds do a lot of important work while wandering'.[64] When Miranda seemingly does not pay attention to Prospero's story at the start of *The Tempest*, for example, 'it may also be that she needs moments of absence to process what she is hearing into her personal narratives of past, present, and future'.[65]

Lyne positions mind-wandering as the site of autonomy and creativity, practices crucial for fostering critical thinking, academic freedom, and originality. He suggests that 'failing' to focus on Shakespeare is not an example of bad learning but rather a way of tapping in to the essential restorative, creative, and generative processes of diversion that our brain/mind needs, and that Shakespeare provokes us to use:

> When we drift away for a moment, or longer, from full attention to a Shakespeare play, we submit more to these essential processes. A playwright might actually benefit from such mind-wandering. Whether watching or reading, those encountering a play should focus on it, but perhaps they also need to have their minds divert, with or without awareness of the wandering, to work out how it relates to them, ideally by telling a little story inwardly about why they like it, learn from it, understand it, and so on. Travels in time and space are characteristic of mind-wandering, but this is not a matter of dispersal; rather, it is about a kind of maintenance, putting knowledge and experience in contact with memories, plans, and narratives of the self.[66]

---

[64] Lyne, 'Shakespeare and the Wandering Mind', 2.
[65] Lyne, 'Shakespeare and the Wandering Mind', 2.
[66] Lyne, 'Shakespeare and the Wandering Mind', 5.

Lyne's reminder to engage the whole bodymind in mind-wandering ('travels in time *and* space', my emphasis) fits with the importance of allowing students to move (or not) in ways that fit their thinking styles: encouraging them to take breaks, move around, and stim. Lyne's reading is particularly attractive to me because it describes mind-wandering as a way of making Shakespeare our *own*, relating it to our past, present, and future. Rather than being shut out, mocked, and blocked from access to Shakespeare, we are able to seize Shakespeare, break him up, wander off and come back to him without feeling that we thereby missed out on some correct, essential Shakespeare experience.

The neurodivergent artist Michelle Attias describes 'mind meandering' as a creative part of the ADHD experience that involves ideas 'spark[ing]' others, 'tripping over emotions and memories, time to sort and heal', and 'time to explore with intensity that which others don't understand or care about'.[67] Attias emphasises the unique directionality of ADHD thought, the challenges involved for ADHD-ers in following normative able-minded directionalities, and how important it is to allow ADHD-ers to make their own connections between ideas no matter how sporadic and radical these may seem to outsiders. Doing so encompasses, she writes, 'a universe of possibility':

> Mind-meandering makes connections between disparate information and seeks non-linear associations which strad- dle a universe of possibility. Mind meandering is where experimentation occurs, where subject matter that is inter- esting can be pursued without a timeline, without direction, without expected outcomes.[68]

Within this vast space of the ADHD universe, Attias maps space and time neurodivergently. She describes the 'geographic place' of ADHD, created

---

[67] Michelle Attias, 'Mind-Meandering as AD(H)D Methodology: An Embodied, Neuroqueer Practice of Art-Making and Resistance in Dialogue with Kurt Cobain's and Lee Lozano's Journals', *Research in Arts and Education* 4 (2020) (pp. 53–85), 64–65.

[68] Attias, 'Mind-Meandering as AD(H)D Methodology', 66.

when a person relinquishes notions of 'right' directions and expected, projected futures.[69] Neurodivergence frequently involves non-normative ways of moving through space and time, from meandering towards developmental 'milestones' at a different pace or angle to other people, to stumbling, stimming, and running out of class. Rosemary Richings signals this in the title of her book on dyspraxia: *Stumbling Through Space and Time*.[70]

Lyne gives a particularly suggestive example of how Shakespeare incorporates distraction into his writing: Canterbury's knotty, complex description of Salique Law in *Henry V* I.i, which can be hard for modern readers or audiences to follow in detail. Lyne argues that Shakespeare's characters may also find it hard to focus on Canterbury's abstruse legal arguments: 'the speech is shaped to allow our minds to drift towards thinking about where the minds of onstage listeners may be drifting, which is a sharp-edged dramatical ploy'.[71] Lyne points out that this is symptomatic of the way in which, throughout *Henry V*, Henry veils the irregularities and nuances in much of what he does in pursuit of power, thereby prompting or at least leaving space for wandering thoughts as audiences and characters muse on what is truly going on in Henry's mind and behaviour.[72] Listeners can react to Canterbury's speech in multiple ways depending on how much they can focus their attention on it at a given moment. It can be a useful speech to listen to in a neurodiverse classroom because there is no 'correct' amount of attention that we are supposed to give the speech; Shakespeare asks us both to focus and not focus on it and we can accept whichever invitation suits us. Students' individual ways of responding to the speech will enable classes to come up with a diverse range of answers to big questions in the play, such as: Is Henry's claim to France so shaky that Canterbury deliberately makes his speech hard to follow? Is there a big gap between modern readers and early modern readers because Shakespeare is assuming that his audience has the skills and knowledge to follow the discussion of Salique law and parse it

[69] Attias, 'Mind-Meandering as AD(H)D Methodology', 67–68.
[70] Rosemary Richings, *Stumbling through Space and Time* (London: Jessica Kingsley, 2022).
[71] Lyne, 'Shakespeare and the Wandering Mind', 10.
[72] Lyne, 'Shakespeare and the Wandering Mind', 12.

point by point? What are the political implications of giving up on this inaccessible speech and deciding not to expend effort listening closely to it and determining whether Canterbury is talking sense?

Lyne notes that Prospero attempts to control other characters' mind-wandering, using threats in order to focus Miranda, Ariel, and Caliban's thoughts to his liking: 'Prospero is wary of divergent mental work, pressing characters back into line, pushing them towards attention, sometimes in vain'.[73] In presenting us with such a tyrannical model of forced focus, the text here invites us to imagine how we might behave differently with our students: rather than viewing an ableist notion of 'focus' as indicative of a good student learning well, we might remove this norm from the classroom. Instead of demanding, Prospero-like, that all students focus on a given topic for a long period of time, we can create opportunities for students to engage in varying ways, such as: creating connections with other ideas and texts/media outside a single Shakespearean text, asserting their right to take movement breaks and leave the classroom and return when they are ready (we might think of this as 'travelling in time and space' rather than inattentiveness), daydreaming, focusing monotropically, and discussing texts dynamically with other students.

Teaching Shakespeare on Crip Time

In *The Winter's Tale* IV.i., Shakespeare dwells on the feeling, and creative and narrative potential, of losing track of time. Time personified enters to tell us that, while we thought just a few minutes had passed, in fact, it has been sixteen years. Time first encourages the audience not to judge them for doing this:

> Impute it not a crime
> To me or my swift passage that I slide
> O'er sixteen years and leave the growth untried
> Of that wide gap, since it is in my power
> To o'erthrow law and in one self-born hour
> To plant and o'erwhelm custom.[74]

---

[73] Lyne, 'Shakespeare and the Wandering Mind', 2.

[74] William Shakespeare, *The Winter's Tale*, ed. Susan Snyder and Deborah Curren-Aquino (Cambridge: Cambridge University Press, 2007), IV.i.1–9.

Time emphasises the disruptive and generative potential of having a sense of time that differs from the norm of clock-time. Though we might feel we have lost out by not fully experiencing the 'wide gap' of 16 years, Time emphasises their 'power', and ability not only to destroy norms but to create new ones: 'To o'erthrow law ... To plant and o'erwhelm custom'. Moreover, Time describes the amazing things that have happened in the gap of time, especially Perdita's development into a graceful and admirable woman: 'Perdita, now grown in grace | Equal with wond'ring' (IV.i.24–5). Time's use of poetic, descriptive language to reclaim the sixteen years means that these years are not 'lost' or 'wasted'; rather, they are the site of growth, fantasy, and future potential.

Shakespeare took an interest in time's variety and creative power in his early plays, too. *The Comedy of Errors* portrays different affective responses to clock time. This play's characters work to an extremely high-stakes deadline: the Duke of Ephesus stipulates that Egeon must find an Ephesian friend to help him pay a fine by 5 pm otherwise he will be beheaded. This plot ultimately involves Egeon's whole estranged family reuniting by the deadline. Some characters benefit from the confusion ensuing from the 5 pm deadline, especially Antipholus of Syracuse who, mistaken for his twin, is handed a gold chain seemingly for free and invited to a free dinner and then bed by a strange woman claiming to be his wife. While Antipholus of Syracuse lives out a certain acquisitive and heterosexual fantasy, Antipholus and Dromio of Ephesus make errors and are victims of others' errors, and end up physically lashed together, facing incarceration. Indeed, *The Comedy of Errors* offers multiple opportunities for neurodivergent readings that reflect the characters' own experiences. For example, Antipholus and Dromio of Syracuse are approached in Ephesus by several people who claim to recognise them and know them intimately; however, Antipholus and Dromio of Syracuse do not recognise their interlocutors and have no memory of the past events they refer to. The characters' inability to tell who is who evokes neurodivergent experiences of not readily recognising people from their faces (often experienced as part of autism and dementia, for instance), as well as the fact that even Shakespeare academics cannot always remember who is whom in a multi-charactered Shakespeare play. Considering *The Comedy of Errors* in this way can give students a detailed understanding of how neurodiverse readers' experiences of time can be in dialogue with characters' experiences of time. This can lead them to consider the relationships between staging (e.g. how long a play was 'supposed' to take), characters' subjectivities, and the structure of Shakespeare's plots in a variety of plays. In *Romeo and Juliet*, for example, Friar Lawrence's time-limited message about Juliet faking her death does not reach Romeo in time. Missing this deadline results in tragedy: both lovers, and Paris, die. How does each character experience time in this play? What if Shakespearean tragedy's very structure is ableist, setting non-negotiable deadlines that are missed with deadly results?

Mind-wandering is a creative and scholarly way of reading. It is also something to accommodate and plan for in the Shakespeare classroom, since institutions hold both students and educators to deadlines regarding class times, coursework, and exams. Several ADHD-ers describe having a different, or little, sense of how time is passing as characteristic of their ADHD identity. In her popular blog 'Black Girl Lost Keys', created to inform, uplift, and motivate Black women with ADHD, René Brooks writes, 'We lose track of time, don't estimate the amount of time we need to finish tasks well, or don't arrive at places on time. We get distracted and spend time on things that ultimately don't matter. It's frustrating!'.[75] Brooks notes difficulties with focusing on one thing for a long period of time, thus 'one of the bedrock pieces of ADHD management is learning how to identify and minimize distractions'.[76] In an episode of the *ADHD Support Talk* podcast series entitled 'Time Blindness and Time Perception Impairment', Tara McGillicuddy and Lynne Edris ask whether it is better for ADHD-ers if their sense of time is adjusted-for (e.g. with flexible deadlines) or whether allies should instead focus on helping the person meet deadlines and have a sense of time more aligned with 'clock time' so that they can get things done 'on time'.[77] The hosts demonstrate the variety

[75] René Brooks, 'ADHD Time Management Troubles: 5 Areas to Attack', https://blackgirllostkeys.com/adhd/adhd-time-management-troubles-5-areas-to-attack/ [Accessed May 2022].

[76] Brooks, 'ADHD Time Management Troubles'.

[77] Tara McGillicuddy and Lynne Edris, 'Time Blindness and Time Perception Impairment', *ADHD Support Talk* www.youtube.com/watch?

of ways that this question can be answered, rather than stipulating a single 'correct' way to help students with ADHD to meet deadlines. Asking students McGillicuddy and Edris's question can help educators to understand which adjustments best help them when it comes to deadlines and timekeeping in their Shakespeare studies. My comments in the paragraph below relate mainly to one of the needs which my students most often express with relation to their studies: the need for chronological flexibility.

Tiffany Stern explains that hourglasses were used to mark time in both early modern playhouses and schoolrooms: marking time in the playhouse visually evoked the marking of time in education.[78] Following up on this connection, students and educators can apply what they have learned about neurodivergent experiences of time through discussing *The Comedy of Errors* to create a classroom that accommodates crip time. When it helps a student to learn, educators can often adjust deadlines and expectations to students' needs. Some deadlines are less flexible, either because we have less power over them (for instance they are externally set exam dates) or because the student has expressed a wish to work to a particular deadline. To support students to meet deadlines and engage fruitfully with Shakespeare in the leadup to a deadline, educators might:

- Include optional exercises in every class that enable students to dialogue and bounce ideas off each other, rather than demanding monolithic focus from every student. These can include collaborative projects and practical exercises involving games and physical movement like those I detailed in Section 1.
- Introduce different activities in each class to make learning less boring for students. Educators might pick from several of the activities in this Element including drawing, acting in parts, and creating and engaging with different media (like Shakespeare podcasts, vlogs, filmed performances).

v=Br5nYhGPCtw [accessed July 2022]. I have kept the podcast title in the creators' own words, though several disabled people and disability studies scholars would dispute the use of the word 'blindness' (a lived disability and identity for many people) as a metaphor for a negative quality.

[78] Tiffany Stern, 'Time for Shakespeare: Hourglasses, Sundials, Clocks, and Early Modern Theatre', *Journal of the British Academy* 3 (2015) (pp. 1–33), 3–4.

- Allow students to make their own connections between ideas. Challenge the academic dictum that there must be a single 'through line' of argument in an essay to make it 'coherent'; ideas can cohere in many ways. Often a stipulation that students write in a 'coherent' or 'organised' way, or something similar to this, is a criterion for success in assessments. Educators might consider how to prepare students well for assessments whilst giving them the tools to critically analyse *what* the assessment is asking of them, *why* it is doing so, and the extent to which this criterion is a neurotypical norm.
- Be flexible and compassionate about whether a student has completed the preparation tasks for the class (e.g. preparatory reading) and refrain from shaming or blaming students who do not complete tasks when they are 'supposed' to.
- Ensure that, even if a student has not completed the preparation tasks, they can still participate in class (this can be as simple as providing an extract on a class handout for students to discuss, which students do not need to have prepared for).
- Stay open to the possibility that students' comments will change the direction of a class, make new connections and introduce new topics of interest to the class.

Educators with more power can ensure that there is a clear, accessible system in place for students to obtain deadline extensions and that neurodivergent conditions are recognised as valid reasons to gain an extension. As I discuss in Section 1, focusing on what students need rather than what conditions they have can be most helpful. For instance, removing requirements that a student have an official diagnosis in order to gain an extension is fairer towards students who need adjustments but are unable to gain a correct diagnosis or who have self-diagnosed.

Educators can support students to meet deadlines by reminding students regularly how much time there is until a deadline, working with students to record deadlines in the way that works best for them (for instance, if a student uses particular Calendar software, supporting them to input deadlines into their system), and offering students a short meeting when they are mid-essay or when planning an assessment to enable them to talk their ideas through and break up the long, boring time spent focusing on one topic. Both McGillicuddy and Edris emphasised that time might be 'a foreign concept' to an ADHD-er; 'it's not my thing', explained Edris. They suggested ways of 'externalising time' that can help ADHD-ers to gain 'a sense of time', which can be adapted in the classroom. These include: having a clock (analogue or digital depending on students' preferences) visible in the classroom/study space so that students can see the hands/digits approaching the hour, including images of clocks on documents to indicate the time allotted to classroom activities, and supporting students to gain a rough sense of how long something usually takes for them as an individual person, in varying circumstances. We might ask students to develop conclusions like, 'it takes me about two hours to read an article and take notes when I'm tired; one hour when I'm wide awake'.

Activity: Giving Francis Power over Time

Returning to the scene with Francis, Hal, and Poins with which I opened this section: what if crip time prevailed in this scene? In *A Winter's Tale*, Time has the power to make time freeze, restart, speed up, and slow down. What if we handed the same power to Francis? In this exercise:

> Ask students to think themselves into Francis's shoes. Perform the scene, and at any point in the scene, the student playing Francis can take control of time. They might 'freeze' Hal and Poins so that Francis can speak at length and in his own time. They might skip over parts of the conversation Francis doesn't want to deal with. What does Francis want to say and do and why? How is temporality working or not working for him in this scene? Is Francis pleased to be reminded by the Vintner that he has work to do (as he has forgotten) or does the Vintner just add more stress to Francis's life?

Educators should never demand that particular students tell the class about their condition, identity, or experience. However, students may spontaneously relate this exercise to their own experiences with focus, distraction, and deadlines. This exercise is primarily designed to open out conversations about distraction and communication in general. It invites students to interpret Francis and what he needs in the moment based on their own different experiences of time, and to learn from each other about the many ways that time figures in a neurodiverse classroom.

Conclusion

In this section, I have argued that there is no single right way to read Shakespeare. How much time, attention, movement, and variety of themes and topics should students bring to bear on the Shakespearean text? However much is right for them. I have demonstrated that Shakespeare's texts are already full of neurodivergent potential as he invites us to read and watch his plays in multiple ways that diverge from ableist norms of focus and time. Moreover, he represents characters who engage with texts, attention, and time in diverging ways, from Canterbury expounding Salique law, to Miranda not focusing as much as Prospero wants her to on his story; from Time making sixteen years pass in a minute, to Francis's clashing interaction with Hal and Poins.

This is distinct from saying that Shakespeare represents particular conditions in his plays: we do not need to diagnose Miranda with ADHD in order to relate her wandering mind meaningfully to her characterisation and to our own experiences with time, selfhood, and attention. In Section 3, I argue that it is unhelpful to try and retrospectively 'diagnose' Shakespearean characters in an uncritical manner. Rather than tying one character to, for example, ADHD experience and thereby implying that this character may represent students with ADHD in our classroom, we can appreciate the multiple ways that multiple readers can engage with Shakespeare. Shakespeare is often understood, as the University of Birmingham's eponymous research project states, to be 'everything to everybody'.[79] This sentiment liberates students to read him dyslexically, autistically, along with the voices they hear, with ADHD, or dementia. However, lingering notions of Shakespeare's role as a great Establishment figure understood only by an elite class of people can be

---

[79] https://everythingtoeverybody.bham.ac.uk/ [accessed August 2022].

used to delegitimise neurodivergent readings (and readings in languages and cultures other than English, readings by working class, BIPOC, and LGBTQ + people, and readings conducted outside academia). We must trust ourselves to have what it takes to interpret Shakespeare. We must trust that the neuro-tools we have are enough. But also, we can trust the text, trust that it has something for us.

3 Shakespeare's Neurodiverse Characters: Beyond Diagnosis

Clear Summary

- Readers and audiences often want to diagnose Shakespearean characters with particular neurodivergent conditions. However, we should do so in a critical way.
- This section discusses the biases and historical changes in the diagnostic process.
- Shakespeare's characters challenge the idea that a diagnosis provides an objective, static label. Instead, diagnosis can be dynamic and fluid, something we can tell different stories about.

At once poisoner and self-proclaimed medic, Iago provokes Othello to 'fall [*sic*.] into a trance' by protractedly persecuting him and then prompting him to imagine Desdemona and Cassio in bed.[80] When Cassio enters to see what has happened, Iago labels Othello's condition: 'My lord is fallen into an epilepsy. | This is his second fit; he had one yesterday' (IV.i.47–8). We have plenty of reasons to mistrust Iago's explanation even though his diagnostic label may be 'correct': Othello may have epilepsy. However, Iago uses this diagnosis to further destroy Othello, and to manipulate readers and audiences against him. Katherine Schaap Williams writes, 'Othello's epileptic fit accomplishes both an apparent revelation of character and a horrifying demonstration of the spectator's diagnostic power to narrate the incapacitated figure'; accordingly, critics

---

[80] William Shakespeare, *Othello*, ed. Norman Sanders (Cambridge: Cambridge University Press, 2018), IV.i.41.SD.

and audiences read it as evidence that Othello is losing his rationality and becoming controlled by emotion:

> Iago has turned the 'trance' into a series of diagnoses that convert the disabling into a truth about Othello's person. Disability accrues social significance far beyond medical contexts as the structure of the scene encourages the audience to understand the fit as evidence of Othello's incapacitation.[81]

Nevertheless, Shakespeare enables us (as Williams has done) to critique the process by which Iago arrives at this label because he shows us the racist, self-serving interests informing it.

We can be fruitfully suspicious about diagnosing any Shakespearean character with a so-called neurodivergent condition. Remi Yergeau argues that, 'autistic people queer the contours of rhetorical containment, of diagnostic fixity'; their argument can apply not just to autism but to all neurodivergence.[82] Aligning herself with queer-theoretical understandings of queerness, Nick Walker describes neuroqueerness as a dynamic verb rather than a static noun, a way of living in the world that cannot be encapsulated by a fixed diagnostic category and which indeed works actively to challenge fixed categories.[83] For Walker, 'neuroqueerness' defies restrictive categories; in the same way that 'we shouldn't allow our conceptions of sexuality and gender to be constrained by the binaristic categories of male and female, or gay and straight', she explains, we shouldn't allow rigid, essentialist diagnostic categories to restrict the way we behave, or prevent us exploring who we are and fulfilling our potential.[84] Walker argues that there is no such

---

[81] Katherine Schaap Williams, *Unfixable Forms* (Ithaca, NY: Cornell University Press, 2021), 168–69.

[82] Remi Yergeau, *Authoring Autism: On Rhetoric and Neurological Queerness* (Durham, NC: Duke University Press, 2018), 140.

[83] 'Neuroqueer is active subversion of both neuronormativity and heteronormativity. Neuroqueer is intentional noncompliance with the demands of normative performance', Walker, *Neuroqueer Heresies*, 175.

[84] Walker, *Neuroqueer Heresies*, 173.

thing as an innate neurotypical brain or neurodivergent brain, though we may be born with a tendency towards behaviours that culture deems neurotypical or neurodivergent, thus some people find it easier and more 'intuitive' to comply with neurotypical standards than others.[85] What is neurotypical in some time-periods and contexts may be considered neurodivergent in others, and vice versa. Diagnostic categories for specific conditions also change over time (over the past 100 years and more since autism was first named, there have been huge, and ongoing, changes in the ingredients for an autism diagnosis). As Valerie Traub argues of early modern sexuality, applying a label like 'lesbian' to an early modern character can give an illusion of knowledge about that character – but it is just an illusion.[86] In this section, I suggest ways of critiquing diagnostic labels in order to gain deeper and more functional knowledge of Shakespeare's neurodivergent characters.

Plenty of Shakespeare's characters look like they might fit into diagnostic frameworks and other recognisable neurodivergent labels. Applying these labels implicates us in notions of 'representation' that might unhelpfully suggest that Shakespeare is presenting us with paradigmatic examples of particular modern diagnostic categories. Falstaff, who has sold his soul to the devil 'for a cup of Madeira and a cold capon's leg' (1 *Henry IV* 1.2.93–4) seems a representation of addiction in all four plays he appears in. Several characters (like Katherine in *Henry VIII*, Joan of Arc in *1 Henry VI*, Brutus in *Julius Caesar*, Posthumus in *Cymbeline*, Richard III, Macbeth and Banquo in *Macbeth*, and the Jailor's Daughter in *Two Noble Kinsmen*) hear voices and/or experience visual hallucinations or what might be interpreted as traumatic flashbacks and intrusive images when they are visited by witches, devils, and the ghosts of dead loved ones. Several characters (like Jacques in *As You Like It*, and Ophelia and Hamlet in *Hamlet*) experience depression and suicidal ideation. The speaker of the *Sonnets* reveals in the final two sonnets that he seems to have syphilis, a disease that can result in neurodivergent effects, like hallucinations. Some characters give us hints that make us wonder if they should have a diagnosis, for instance when actors portray Malvolio as unable to smile in

[85] Walker, *Neuroqueer Heresies*, 181–82.
[86] Valerie Traub, *Thinking Sex with the Early Moderns* (Pennsylvania, PA: Pennsylvania University Press, 2015), 1, 13, 34.

a 'normal' way (his smile seems too pinched or exaggerated by neurotypical standards), and when Malvolio himself describes how he rehearses facial expressions before they are needed (practicing 'quenching [his] familiar smile with an austere control of regard'), we might wonder, is he autistic?[87] When they see Lady Macbeth compulsively washing her hands, students often wonder (not uninfluenced by stereotypes linking OCD with handwashing) – did she have OCD? Does King Lear have dementia? Is Helena in *All's Well* a sociopath? The questions pile up.

The literature on neurodiverse conditions in Shakespeare is rich, and growing. To name just a few examples, Avi Mendelson traces the psychological effects of rabies in *King Lear*, Alice Equestri and Bridget Bartlett analyse Shakespearean fools and madmen in the context of intellectual disability, and (as I discuss in this Section) Justin Shaw examines Othello's epilepsy through a framework of race and disability.[88] Lianne Habinek reads Hamlet as having head trauma, arguing that his act of wiping memories from his brain can be understood both as following the precepts of early modern memory manuals (which advised removing unnecessary thoughts) and as brain injury.[89] Kelsey Ridge argues that Othello may have suffered a traumatic brain injury in war

---

[87] William Shakespeare, *Twelfth Night*, ed. Elizabeth Story Donno, 3rd ed. (Cambridge: Cambridge University Press, 2017), II.v.54–55.

[88] Avi Mendelson, 'Enabling Rabies in *King Lear*', in, Leslie Dunn, ed., *Performing Disability in Early Modern English Drama* (New York: Palgrave, 2021), 161–83; Alice Equestri, 'Shakespeare and the Construction of Intellectual Disability: The Case of Touchstone', *Disability Studies Quarterly* 40(4) (2020) and '"This cold night will turn us all into fools and madmen": Shakespeare's Witty Fools and the Border between Idiocy and Mental Illness', *Cahiers Élisabéthains* 99 (2019), 23–32; Bridget Bartlett, 'Macbeth's Idiot and Faulkner's Compsons', *Borrowers and Lenders* 14(2) (2023), 139–42; Justin Shaw, '"Rub Him about the Temples": Othello, Disability, and the Failures of Care', *Early Theatre* 22(2) (2019), 171–84.

[89] Lianne Habinek, 'Altered States: *Hamlet* and Early Modern Head Trauma', in Laurie Johnson Evelyn Tribble, and John Sutton, eds., *Embodied Cognition and Shakespeare's Theatre* (London: Routledge, 2018) (pp. 195–215), 197 and passim.

which 'puddled his clear spirit'.[90] Lindsey Row-Heyveld suggests that the slowness and delay which characterise early modern revenge tragedies including *Hamlet* can be attributed to the avengers' intellectual disability and madness, allowing audiences to 'indulge' in madness (as it absolves the revenger of guilt) as well as condemn it, rendering the avenger 'both guilty and innocent'.[91] Olivia Henderson, Sonya Freeman Loftis, and Lisa Ulevich examine autistic traits in Shakespeare's characters.[92]

Out in the wild, the diagnostic process is all too often imbricated with bias. Stijn Vanheule shows that DSM diagnostic criteria were developed in a biased way that makes the DSM a 'rigidly North American instrument' rather than a cosmopolitan one; Vanheule details that the DSM fails adequately to theorise its (in)applicability to other cultures and was shaped by the profit-motives of specific pharmaceutical companies.[93] Gender, class, LGBTQ+ status, and race impact on people's access to diagnosis, and the types of diagnosis (if any) they are likely to receive. In an essay on racial biases in US diagnoses, Danielle Hairston et al. explain that these biases influence both clinicians' and patients' expectations of the clinical relationship, the type of diagnosis offered, which diagnostic criteria clinicians attend to, and the types of care they provide and mandate.[94] Hairston

---

[90] Kelsey Ridge, *Shakespeare's Military Spouses and Twenty-First-Century Warfare* (London: Routledge, 2021), Chapter 1.

[91] Lindsey Row-Heyveld, 'Antic Dispositions: Mental and Intellectual Disabilities in Early Modern Revenge Tragedy', in Alison Hobgood and David Houston-Wood, eds., *Recovering Disability in Early Modern England* (Columbus, OH: Ohio State University Press, 2013) (pp. 73–87), 84 and passim.

[92] Olivia Henderson, '"Like a Dull Actor Now I Have Forgot My Part" Coriolanus and Shakespearean Autism', *Shakespeare Studies* 50 (2022), 126–52; Sonya Freeman Loftis and Lisa Ulevich, 'Obsession/Rationality/Agency: Autistic Shakespeare', in Sujata Iyengar, ed., *Disability, Health, and Happiness in the Shakespearean Body* (London: Routledge, 2014) 58–75.

[93] Stijn Vanheule, *Diagnosis and the DSM* (London: Palgrave, 2014), 57.

[94] Danielle Hairston, Tresha A. Gibbs, Shane Shucheng Wong, and Ayana Jordan, 'Clinician Bias in Diagnosis and Treatment', in Morgan Medlock Derri Shtasel, Nhi-Ha T. Trinh, and David R. Williams, eds., *Racism and Psychiatry: Contemporary Issues and Interventions* (Cham: Humana Cham, 2019), 105–37.

et al. recommend cultivating an environment where clinicians and patients are both aware of racial biases and can openly discuss the impacts of these biases on treatment. Educators might encourage students to reflect on the lability of diagnostic criteria and the class, race, and gender biases inherent within diagnosis by reading work by Vanheule and Hairston et al. Classes might read Dolly Sen's creative, parodic, funny, and poignant challenge to diagnostic criteria and celebration of mad culture, *DSM 69*. Sen writes that the DSM 'aims to pathologise all things human'; it is

> supposed to be a book on the classification of mental disor-
> ders, but reads more like an Argos catalogue, where you may
> or may not get what you ordered, handed to you in boxes by
> people who don't know you, and are just waiting for the next
> person in line to be a bastard to. The only difference is there is
> no warranty when they break your soul.[95]

Educators might trace how diagnostic criteria for different conditions have altered over the decades, casting doubt on the notion that there is such thing as a trans-historically valid 'diagnosis' that we can apply unproblematically to Shakespeare's characters. These discussions can raise fruitful questions in the classroom about how diagnosis is inflected by biases both in Shakespeare's time and our own. David Sterling Brown explains how Shakespeare relies on ideas of whiteness and blackness to construct Hamlet's gender, 'depicting unmanliness as a kind of monstrous blackness'.[96] This might prompt students to wonder, following Brown, how race and gender intertwine with Hamlet's melancholy. Returning to Malvolio, we might claim him as autistic because of the traits I described earlier in this Section. In so doing, it is most useful to interrogate the ways in

---

[95] Dolly Sen, *DSM 69: Dolly Sen's Manual of Psychiatric Disorder* (London: Eleusinian Press, 2016), 3. I am grateful to Hamja Ahsan for introducing me to Sen's work.

[96] David Sterling Brown, 'Code Black: Whiteness and Unmanliness in *Hamlet*', in Lucy Munro and Sonia Massai, ed., *Hamlet: The State of Play* (London: Bloomsbury Arden, 2021), (pp. 101–28), 105.

which Malvolio's maleness and what we might read as (highly!) aspirational middle-class status feed in to our learned stereotypes of what an autistic person most often looks like, and how they challenge them.

Reading Shakespeare alongside accounts of lived experiences of different disabilities – for instance, pairing *King Lear* with Jennifer Bute and Wendy Mitchell's accounts of living with dementia – might prompt students to ask: what kinds of texts are these? Where do they come from? What are their aims? Can they be compared? What is at stake in comparing them?[97] Links between modern and Shakespearean understandings of neurodivergence can be mutually informative, such as Ridge's use, in *Shakespeare's Military Spouses*, of interviews with present day military spouses to understand issues in Shakespeare's plays like adultery, PTSD, and queer relationships.

For interrogating what diagnosis and difference might have meant to Shakespeare, and how they were inflected by a patient's gender, race, and other positionalities, students might read Sujata Iyengar's *Shakespeare's Medical Language: A Dictionary*, and work by scholars including Mary Ann Lund, Erin Sullivan, and Stephanie Shirilan elucidating early modern depression and melancholy.[98] The contributors to Iyengar's edited collection, *Disability, Health and Happiness in the Shakespearean Body*, deal with a range of topics that integrate social identities and disability, such as Amrita Dhar's analysis of blindness and servitude. Equestri discusses how financial and social disability intertwined; begging and not managing money well could contribute to the notion that someone was an 'idiot', excluding the individual from society but also 'giving alternative ways to emerge'.[99]

[97] Wendy Mitchell, *What I Wish People Knew about Dementia: From Someone Who Knows* (London: Bloomsbury, 2022); Jennifer Bute, *Dementia from the Inside: A Doctor's Personal Journal of Hope* (London: SPCK, 2018).

[98] Sujata Iyengar, *Shakespeare's Medical Language: A Dictionary* (London: Bloomsbury, 2014); Mary Ann Lund, *A User's Guide to Melancholy* (Cambridge: Cambridge University Press, 2021); Erin Sullivan, *Beyond Melancholy* (Oxford: Oxford University Press, 2016); Stephanie Shirilan, *Robert Burton and the Transformative Powers of Melancholy* (London: Routledge, 2016).

[99] Alice Equestri, *Literature and Intellectual Disability in Early Modern England* (London: Routledge, 2021), 76.

This emergence includes characters describing their own neurodivergence and neurodivergent experiences. Equestri writes, for instance, that the Shakespearean fool 'plays the double role as a reader of disability and the disabled'.[100] Lindsey Row-Heyveld's book *Dissembling Disability* helps us to contextualise the ways in which characters who feign neurodiversity (like Poor Tom and, potentially, Hamlet) operate in terms of early modern ideas of performed, dissembled disability.

Such discussions can enable students to appreciate 'neurodivergent conditions' not as rigidly fixed categories but as stories open to explanation, changing over time, and flexibly and ludically open to interpretation in the classroom. Instead of asking, if Malvolio is autistic 'enough', or if Lear 'counts' as having dementia, students can ask critical questions about what diagnosis might do to Shakespearean characters, and what potentials these characters offer for talking *back* to diagnoses and stereotypes, as well as all the shifting, multiple factors in play constellating around any diagnosis of disability. Sharon Barnartt's edited collection, *Disability as a Fluid State*, emphasises that a fluid relationship obtains between impairment and disability, with gender, class, race, and age also in play. Mary Jo Deegan writes that ableist societal norms and expectations determine what counts as normal and what is a disability.[101] Schaap Williams argues that we should destabilise the idea that 'disability secures knowledge about who a person is from how a body functions'.[102] Diagnostic criteria about neurodivergent conditions do not offer us secure knowledge about who a person or Shakespearean character is. By critically analysing the diagnostic process itself students can engage with neurodivergence in this more liberatory way, what Williams calls 'unfixing' disability.

Even when we do apply diagnostic criteria, Othello's 'trance' can be read in several ways, from Avi Mendelson's research into how Shakespeare draws on Islamophobic narratives describing the Prophet as epileptic to

---

[100] Equestri, 'This Cold Night', 31.

[101] Mary Jo Deegan, '"Feeling Normal" and "Feeling Disabled"', in Sharon Barnartt, ed., *Disability as a Fluid State* (Bingley: Emerald Group, 2010), 25–48.

[102] Schaap Williams, *Unfixable Forms*, 2.

Ridge's suggestion that Othello has sustained a TBI (traumatic brain injury).[103] Shaw draws on Piepzna-Samarasinha's idea of 'care webs', which I discussed in Section 1, to argue for 'an ethical care that begins with and is oriented through race and disability'.[104] He traces how Cassio and Iago deploy Iago's three diagnoses of Othello's trance (epilepsy, lethargy, madness) to suit themselves, both by feigning ignorance when it suits them and claiming to know Othello and thereby claiming proximity to his power. Cassio surveys Othello's dead body and states it 'poisons sight', simultaneously claiming the role of Governor of Cyprus for himself. Shaw writes, 'Cassio's elegiac response to Othello's death then becomes a confirmation of what he knew rather than a confirmation of what he did not'.[105] As Shaw explains, once Iago and Cassio have 'diagnosed' Othello, their claims to know him become less about genuinely caring for Othello and more about their own attempts to get ahead in the power-systems of Cyprus and Venice. Shaw analyses the role of race, white mediocrity, knowledge and ignorance, failures of care, and systems of anti-black surveillance both in *Othello* in its original early modern context and in police officers' abhorrent racist murders of Black US citizens in our present day and living memory. In the remainder of this section, I suggest two classroom exercises students might engage in to critique gendered Shakespearean diagnoses.

Activity: Diagnosing La Pucelle

In *1 Henry VI* I.ii, the French nobles test Joan la Pucelle's claim to supernatural power in what I read as a diagnosis scene. Readers and audiences may respond to Joan's avowed experiences of hearing voices and seeing visions as an invitation to diagnose her. If Shakespeare does extend such an

---

103 Avi Mendelson, 'Shakespeare and Mad Activism', talk at St Anne's College Oxford, 12 June 2022. A summary of Mendelson's talk is in the pamphlet *Sunglasses on Bright Days* printed by Neurodiversity at Oxford, unnumbered, fols 31–33. neurodiversityoxford.web.ox.ac.uk/files/sunglassesonbrightdays bookletpdf [accessed March 2023].

104 Shaw, 'Rub Him about the Temples', 172.

105 Shaw, 'Rub Him about the Temples', 178.

invitation, he simultaneously invites us to critique the diagnostic process. The French nobles test Joan's insight and intuition by attempting to trick her: the impoverished King of Naples Reignier pretends to be Charles the Dauphin (the heir to the French throne, whom Joan has come to see). Dauphin tests Joan's bodily abilities by fighting her and judges her spiritual authenticity throughout the encounter. Simultaneously, the men test how Joan responds to flirtation and sexual or marital proposition, inviting her to assert or deny her chastity and womanhood. On these gendered exchanges, the men base gendered judgements about Joan's suitability as their spiritual and martial leader. As in many diagnostic situations, then, gender-biases and power are in play. However, it is not as simple as saying that the French nobles wield their classed and gendered power over Joan, obliging her to answer their questions and court their favour:

CHARLES: Reignier, stand thou as dauphin in my place;
            Question her proudly; let thy looks be stern;
            By this means shall we sound what skill she hath.

Enter [BASTARD and] JOAN [LA] PUCELLE

REIGNIER: [*AS CHARLES*] Fair maid, is't thou wilt do these wondrous
            feats?

PUCELLE: Reignier, is't thou that thinkest to beguile me?
            Where is the dauphin? [*To Charles*] Come, come from
            behind;
            I know thee well, though never seen before.
            Be not amazed: there's nothing hid from me.
            In private will I talk with thee apart.
            Stand back, you lords, and give us leave awhile.

REIGNIER: [*TO ALENÇON AND BASTARD*]
            She takes upon her bravely at first dash.
            [*The Lords withdraw*]

PUCELLE: Dauphin, I am by birth a shepherd's daughter,
            My wit untrain'd in any kind of art.
            Heaven and our Lady gracious hath it pleased
            To shine on my contemptible estate.
            Lo, whilst I waited on my tender lambs,

> And to sun's parching heat displayed my cheeks,
> God's mother deignèd to appear to me
> And, in a vision full of majesty,
> Will'd me to leave my base vocation
> And free my country from calamity;
> Her aid she promised and assured success.
> In complete glory she reveal'd herself –
> And whereas I was black and swart before,
> With those clear rays which she infused on me,
> That beauty am I blest with, which you may see.
> Ask me what question thou canst possible,
> And I will answer unpremeditated;
> My courage try by combat, if thou dar'st,
> And thou shalt find that I exceed my sex;
> Resolve on this: thou shalt be fortunate,
> If thou receive me for thy warlike mate.

CHARLES: Thou hast astonished me with thy high terms.
> Only this proof I'll of thy valour make:
> In single combat thou shalt buckle with me,
> And if thou vanquishest, thy words are true;
> Otherwise I renounce all confidence.[106]

Note that, after Reignier and Dauphin's failed attempt to gain the upper hand through their identity-swap, it is Joan who sets the terms of their diagnosis. It is Joan who suggests that Dauphin test her through martial combat, and Joan who suggests a prospect of martial partnership with Dauphin that might include sex or romance when she offers to be his 'warlike mate'. Though Joan offers to submit to a variety of tests and 'answer unpremeditated' any question Dauphin asks, Dauphin rejects this option and chooses physical combat as the only test he needs. This exchange upends certain expectations about what a diagnosis might be, that is, a powerful man imposing his own criteria on a structurally disadvantaged

---

[106] William Shakespeare, *The First Part of King Henry VI*, ed. Michael Hattaway (Cambridge: Cambridge University Press, 1990), I.ii.61–97.

woman. Dauphin initially aimed to test Joan through formidable questions, requiring Reignier to 'question her proudly'. However, once Joan is in the room, her behaviour and her story begin to affect the diagnostic process. Joan presents herself rather than Dauphin as the successful investigator ('there's nothing hid from me') and takes control of the space, time, and participants in their interview: 'Come, come from behind . . . In private will I talk with thee apart'. Dauphin ultimately selects his preferred diagnostic tool (physical combat rather than questioning Joan) based on his shifting interpretation of her while they talk.

When Joan vanquishes Dauphin in the fight and refuses his offer of sexual or marital partnership (at least until she has 'chasèd' all his 'foes' away, I.ii.115), Dauphin prostrates himself before her. Styling himself her 'thrall', he compares her to the holy Prophet Muhammad (though 'Mahomet's' dove is too peaceful a symbol for warlike Joan) and suggests that she stands out amid some of the most renowned women in Christian history:

> Was Mahomet inspirèd with a dove?
> Thou with an eagle art inspirèd then.
> Helen, the mother of great Constantine,
> Nor yet Saint Philip's daughters were like thee.
> Bright star of Venus, fall'n down on the earth,
> How may I reverently worship thee enough? (I.ii.117, 140–6)

Turning his gaze xenophobically upon the French and their heroine, Shakespeare does not allow this reverence to go unchallenged or unmocked. Reignier and Alençon undercut this reverence with disparaging sexual comments about why Dauphin and Joan's exchange is taking so long. Figuring this exchange as a religious confession (a situation not entirely distinct from diagnosis given its focus on cause, symptoms, duration, severity, and cure) that dissolves into a sexual scenario, Alençon suggests that Dauphin 'shrives this woman to her smock' (I.ii.119). Here, Alençon imagines Dauphin's close analysis of Joan involving sexual undertones as in an attempt to know her, he/she/they remove her clothes until she is wearing only the garment typically worn closest to the skin: a smock. Reignier places the onus on Joan, implying that her words serve not to elucidate her spiritual and psychological condition but rather to seduce Dauphin: 'These women are shrewd tempters with their tongues' (I.ii.123). From Joan's first appearance, Shakespeare injects an explicit theme of gendered disparagement into situations where characters are otherwise listening carefully to Joan, her words and physical strength holding weight in how powerful men such as Dauphin judge her.

Introducing this scene in the above way to students enables me not to stop at the dangerously closed question 'what might you diagnose La Pucelle with?', but to invite more original critical analysis by asking, 'how does diagnosis take place in this scene'? As part of this activity, students could close-read a list of diagnostic criteria, supported by selections from works discussing diagnosis like Sen's and Vaheule's, and ask the following questions of this scene from *1 Henry VI*: Who has power here? Who is speaking? Who can speak back? What is not being said? What is this text similar to? Which factors beyond neurodivergence (e.g. gender, race, class) are in play? This activity enables students to gain a more precise handle on one particular set of technical terminology they might apply to a Shakespearean text: diagnostic terminology. Simultaneously, it supports students to accrue relevant knowledge of historical and critical traditions surrounding this terminology, relating closely to a Shakespeare play.

My aim in analysing Shakespeare's representation of La Pucelle with students is not for students to feel they have 'diagnosed' La Pucelle but rather to encourage students to critique the process of diagnosis, particularly in terms of how it relates to power, stereotype, and history. In so doing, students are empowered to assess different methodologies for analysing Shakespearean texts. Students might consider their own position when they are wielding diagnostic knowledge and power against/upon characters who can't talk back. Do they think a version of the Goldwater rule (the rule that psychiatrists should not diagnose a public figure they have never met, and whose mental health they do not have permission to discuss) applies when we are talking about early modern authors or actors? What about Shakespearean characters? Do they see any similarities between the process of diagnosis and literary criticism? What does it mean to work in one discipline like literary criticism, but draw from another area of knowledge (psychology and medicine) – what kinds of assumptions do we make about which disciplines have more access to truth, or power? These questions guide students to consider more judiciously which critical methods they use and why. Using literary critical skills to close read a list of diagnostic criteria enables students to see what insights their skills as literary scholars can bring to other disciplines. A list of diagnostic criteria is not the only kind of text that works well in this exercise: close reading the school or university's accessibility statement (if it exists), or a piece of journalism about neurodivergence, or a political document from a resource like the UK's Hansard repository of parliamentary debates, alongside *1 Henry VI* II.i can all work well. To access Hansard, students can visit hansard.parliament.uk and search for keywords like 'disability' or 'autism' to find relevant debates.

In order to relate this close analysis of II.i to a broader understanding of *1 Henry VI*, students might trace the effects of Shakespeare putting La Pucelle up for diagnosis. Does II.i lay the ground for the English soldiers' more overtly and violently misogynistic and xenophobic treatment of her? In *1 Henry VI* V.iv, the English mock Joan's statements that she is pregnant, and her naming of different men as her baby's father, in her attempts to escape execution. Rather than a divinely inspired prophetess, they call her a 'minister of hell', 'vicious', 'wicked and vile' (V.iv.16, 35, 93). Students might reflect on the ways in which the histories of queerness and gender non-conformity have long been intertwined with the histories of mental illness, and how tests of 'normalcy' have historically encompassed the patient's sexuality and gender expression as well as their psychology. Conversations might range to gender and sexuality in performance – might Joan be an LGBTQ+ person, for example, as they were in the Globe's 2022 *I Joan* which presents them as non-binary? In her (to return to Shakespeare's pronouns for Joan) first encounter with Dauphin, cited above, Joan describes her religious vision in racialised terms, associating her martial prowess and spiritually 'blessed' state with a change in her skin colour. Contrasting her previous 'black and swart' appearance with her new 'bless'd' 'beauty', bestowed by the Virgin Mary's 'clear' (bright but also colourless, transparent) beams, Joan repeats the common Renaissance trope of Christian conversion or election as the literal whitening of dark skin deemed ugly.[107] Students might inquire into the ways in which Joan attempts to avoid an undesired diagnosis by presenting herself as beautiful and white.

Educators might choose to centre this class, which analyses La Pucelle's descriptions of herself, around the theme of storytelling and the creativity of neurodivergent writing. Sen's response to delusions of being the Messiah was to speak back creatively to her diagnosis, and to the DSM. As well as publishing *DSM 69*, she created, for instance, a website experiencing psychosis which thinks it is Jesus and hears voices.[108] Sen argues for the power of creativity to challenge diagnostic criteria and also to make sense of her own experience in ways that diagnostic and clinical language cannot, 'words like disorder, pathology, false beliefs don't explain my experience or help me make sense of them: creativity does'.[109] In *The Wounded Storyteller* (1995), Arthur Frank emphasises the importance of narrative, storytelling, and creativity to disabled experience, advocating for speaking about and through wounded bodies rather than allowing oneself to be seen simply as the 'victim' of disease or disability. As Frank notes, when one person finds their voice, others are helped to find theirs too, citing literary examples of wounded storytellers like Tiresias. In this vein, students might ask how the creativity of Shakespeare's writing and the creative possibilities of performance enable Joan to speak back to diagnostic categories relating to hallucinations and delusions. They might explore the literary (and in the case of the Oedipus complex, Shakespearean) roots of diagnoses like the Oedipus and Electra complexes.

As an alternative to diagnostic criteria, students might draw on 'own stories' narratives: texts where neurodivergent people talk about their neurodivergent experiences in their own words. They might read Joan's religious visions and conversations with devils (though when they appear onstage in V. iii, the devils don't speak back) alongside the materials in Angela Woods

---

[107] For analysis of this trope see Dennis Austin Britton, *Becoming Christian: Race, Reformation, and Early Modern English Romance* (New York: Fordham University Press, 2014).

[108] Dolly Sen, http://internetbreakdown.com/ [accessed August 2022].

[109] Sen, *DSM 69*, 8.

et al.'s Hearing the Voice project at Durham, integrating historical studies such as Christopher Cook's *Christians Hearing Voices* which emphasises the centrality of voice hearing to religious experiences in Joan's religion, Christianity.[110] Very often, Shakespeare's Joan is speaking under threat. When the French nobles use their power to 'test' her, Joan's responses may be shaped by an apprehension that if she fails the test, the Dauphin will start to treat her as his sexual property. When she is captured by the English, Joan's claims about her experiences and selfhood are desperate ones, as she attempts to evade execution. Her situation is extreme, but concerns for one's survival, people-pleasing, and attempts to live up to the expectations and stereotypes of the person doing the diagnosing can shape the ways in which neurodivergent people respond to diagnostic questioning. Sometimes the best or safest answer is not always the most honest one. Students might conduct an exercise similar to that detailed in Section 2 with Francis: what might Joan say about her experiences if she was in a safe environment, and given time and space to speak? Is it possible to know?

Wounded Storytellers: Tracing Margaret
Diagnoses don't have absolute power to fix us in place; human beings develop and grow over time. Adults with autism and ADHD frequently find that services are tailored more to children with those 'conditions' (or, rather, those children's parents) and not adjusted to the needs of adults who have longer experience of living as a neurodivergent person, or who are experiencing the specifically adult life-event that is late diagnosis. The relaxed film showings for autistic people in my local cinemas have tended to show children's films, for example. Rather than diagnosis offering a static be-all and end-all label, humans can have a changing relation to diagnoses throughout their lives, and in different contexts. Tracing a person's changing life-story thus enables further critical analysis of ideas about diagnosis. Queen Margaret, Reignier's daughter, who appears in all three *Henry VI* plays and in *Richard III*, is a good example to analyse; not only do Shakespeare and (in the *Henry VI* plays) his co-author Thomas Nashe trace a large swathe of Margaret's life in their plays, they also show her

---

[110] https://hearingthevoice.org/ [accessed August 2022].

responding to different judgements about her (sexed, gendered, classed, ethnic) bodymind over the course of her life.

Tracing Margaret's story across these four plays enables us to root understandings of neurodiversity in Margaret's personal, individual story rather than in an alienating language of diagnosis. Shakespeare introduces Margaret when an inept and somewhat distracted Suffolk makes her his prisoner, and decides to offer her to Henry as a bride, in *1 Henry VI*. Margaret's capture can be played in a rather light-hearted way as Suffolk is rapt with her beauty to the extent that she needs to prompt him to ask her for a ransom (V.iii.73–7). However, their seeming civility does not mean that the experience is not traumatic or distressing to Margaret. Though Henry seems unconditionally to love Margaret, the English nobles are against her because she does not bring a large dowry and because they deem her too low born and the terms of her marriage detrimental to English expansionist interests. In this hostile court environment, Suffolk is on Margaret's side, supporting her in a style shaped by his vengeful and machinating courtly personality; for example, he ruins the careers of the Duke and Duchess of Gloucester when the Duchess plots against Margaret. In *2 Henry VI*, Margaret traumatically loses this support when Suffolk is killed and she receives, and seems to handle, Suffolk's severed head. She fears her grief might alter her mind negatively, making it weak ('soften[ed]' and 'degenerate'), thus she deliberately mixes her grief with vengeful anger:

> Oft have I heard that grief softens the mind
> And makes it fearful and degenerate;
> Think therefore on revenge and cease to weep.
> But who can cease to weep and look on this?
> Here may his head lie on my throbbing breast:
> But where's the body that I should embrace?[111]

Beginning quite quickly after Suffolk's death, and for the remainder of *2 Henry VI*, Margaret makes political interventions and decisions, fiercely

---

[111] William Shakespeare, *The Second Part of King Henry VI*, ed. Michael Hattaway (Cambridge: Cambridge University Press, 1991), IV.iv.1–6.

defending Henry's crown from the Yorkists. Is this a product of her grief-
ful revenge? In *3 Henry VI* I.iv, Margaret's fierceness becomes cruelty when
she torments York before she and Clarence stab him to death: she dresses
York in a paper crown and offers him a napkin soaked in his son Rutland's
blood to wipe his tears.

Both suffering and perpetrating cruelty no doubt leave their mark on
Margaret. Though the men surrounding her note that she seems unmoved
whilst she tortures York, contrasting her to her tearful ally Northumberland,
Margaret's stony face could be as much a product of her own shock and
suffering as it is a sign of a lack of compassion. York's tears for Rutland
provoke even his enemy Northumberland to cry, whereas, York says,
Margaret's 'face is vizard-like, unchanging, | Made impudent with use of
evil deeds'.[112] 'Impudent' – lacking shame – has potential sexual connota-
tions, particularly as Margaret shows the ultimate disdain for York's children
and family life. If Margaret is shameless in her violent treatment of York,
York implies, is she sexually shameless in her treatment of Henry, not caring
to be a good wife and mother? York adduces that she is fascinatingly ugly (*3
Henry VI* I.iv.128–33). Combined with her stony, mask-like face, this suggests that Margaret is a Medusa-like figure in York's mind: a killing woman
who numbs both herself and others with her cruelty, fascinatingly and
chillingly different from the ideal. Strikingly, Margaret allows York to insult
her in a long monologue before she kills him; she drinks in his words as he
insults her birth, her appearance, and her claim to the throne, and calls her
cruel and emotionless (I.iv.111–49). Her emotional difference leads him to
describe her as no true woman: 'Women are soft, mild, pitiful, and flexible: |
Thou stern, obdurate, flinty, rough, remorseless' (I.iv.141–2). For York,
a woman who is traumatised, and cruel, and numbed, is not a woman.

In *Richard III*, Margaret both becomes and resists becoming what York
says she is: obsessed to the last with her family's claim to the throne, but
simultaneously replete with emotion as she weeps and rages. At the end of
3 Henry VI, V.v, Shakespeare inflicts further trauma on Margaret when
Richard kills her son Edward in front of her. Experiencing for herself

---

[112] William Shakespeare, *The Third Part of King Henry VI*, ed. Michael Hattaway
(Cambridge: Cambridge University Press, 1993), I.iv.116–17.

a version of what she did to York, Margaret truly breaks down and cannot (as she did after Suffolk's death) channel her anger and grief into impactful political action. She begs for death but, in what may be misplaced compassion or a desire to torment her more, Edward and Elizabeth tell Richard not to harm Margaret. Though they say they have done enough to her, and whatever their motivations for not acceding to her desire to die, Edward and Elizabeth inflict further pain on Margaret: she is left living and tormented by her lover, son, and husband's deaths without the relief of her own death.

Tracking Margaret's characterisation over time enables students to track her non-normative behaviours and expressions of emotion across plays. Students can note the role of others' cruelty and trauma at turning points in her life, and the effects of these. Students can examine Margaret as a literary creation, embodied by different performers. Students may indeed decide that Margaret is diagnosable, with PTSD, for instance. However, reading Margaret, students can appreciate the fluid, autonomous way that characters challenge, exceed, and grow through and beyond particular label-able states of being, as well as the personal histories they attach to these labels.

Conclusion

Rather than matching Shakespearean characters up to diagnoses, this section has suggested encouraging students to speak back to diagnostic categories, and to appreciate the ways in which Shakespeare's characters are already doing so. Shakespeare, and crucially, our classroom discussions of his works, can provide us with vocabulary, ideas, and models that enable us to critique the diagnostic process, its history, and its impacts. Both literature and diagnosis can potentially help us to make sense of our world; often they do so in conversation with each other. Centring crip authority, creativity, and literary theory as we grapple with scientific language is in itself a radical act given the threats to devalue literary readings, crip authority, and creativity. The act of reading together – and its power to create a more graceful, inclusive present and future for Shakespeare studies – is the subject of the final section in this Element.

Conclusion. 'What's Past Is Prologue': Neurodiverse Futures

Clear Summary

- If we are not disabled and neurodivergent already, we will probably become disabled and neurodivergent in the future.
- Reading and analysing literature can help us to imagine, and then put into practice, more socially just futures for neurodivergent people.
- This Element ends with a toolkit of resources (actions, books, and websites) that educators can use when teaching Shakespeare and neurodiversity.

From 'Mere Oblivion' to Neurodivergent Joy

and then the justice,
In fair round belly with good capon lined,
With eyes severe and beard of formal cut,
Full of wise saws and modern instances –
And so he plays his part; the sixth age shifts
Into the lean and slippered pantaloon,
With spectacles on nose and pouch on side,
His youthful hose well saved – a world too wide
For his shrunk shank – and his big manly voice,
Turning again toward childish treble, pipes
And whistles in his sound; last scene of all
That ends this strange eventful history
Is second childishness and mere oblivion,
Sans teeth, sans eyes, sans taste, sans everything.[113]

Jacques' description of the seven ages of man in *As You Like It* traces the slip from the cognitively abled Justice to the loss of rhetorical gravity as the man's bodymind changes into a 'pantaloon' (a lean, foolish, feeble old man)

[113] William Shakespeare, *As You Like It*, ed. Michael Hattaway (Cambridge: Cambridge University Press, 2021), II.vii.153–66.

and finally experiences a kind of dementia. Reaching this final stage, Jacques codes the man's thought and life as non-thought and non-life: a memoryless 'second childishness and mere oblivion' lacking the senses and bodily powers that had hitherto played a leading role in the 'eventful history' of the man's life. Jacques knows that if we live long enough, if we are not already disabled and neurodivergent, we will probably become disabled and neurodivergent. Strokes, dementia, acquired mental health conditions, side-effects of physical illnesses and their treatments (such as chemo brain), and changes in norms about who 'counts' as neurotypical can all render us neurodivergent at any point in our lives.

Our individual futures are in all likelihood ones where we are neurodivergent. The future of our planet is – despite states, organisations, and individuals attempting to 'cure' our neurodivergences and screen them out antenatally – likely to be neurodivergent because neurodivergent people are likely to continue to be born and exist in the future. A neurodivergent future filled with the differing kinds of reading, creativity, and communicating I have described in this Element is not just something we should simply tolerate but something we should actively work towards and allow to flourish. Literature enables us to engage in what Piepzna-Samarasinha evocatively calls, 'dreaming disabled futures'.[114] Part of this might involve conversations about our fears for the future of care for neurodivergent people in the places we call home.

Thankfully, we are students and teachers of literature, a medium which encourages us to speculate and imagine the future, as wildly as possible. Literary analysis can give us permission to dream big and expand our horizons beyond the limits society places on what we can ask for, imagine, and desire.[115] Before I read Wendy Mitchell's account of her young-onset dementia, *What I Wish People Knew About Dementia*, my view of dementia was dominated by fears and stereotypes. After mulling over Mitchell's

---

[114] Leah Lakshmi Piepzna-Samarasinha, *The Future Is Disabled* (Vancouver: Arsenal Pulp Press, 2022), 154–64, 168–74.

[115] I use the word 'imagine' in a broad sense which encompasses any kind of wishful planning, creativity, and speculation. Narrowly, 'imagine' suggests creating specifically an image in one's mind. However, several people cannot 'see' images in their minds, or prefer not to think in this way.

book – which explains how she experiences the world and is filled with tips for allies, and tales of her sadness, joy, frustrations, immense creativity, and compassion for others – my fears were replaced with hope. Even though the stories Shakespeare offers about neurodivergence are not always particularly joyful, the ways in which they spark imaginative neurodivergent interpretations and communities almost always offer students opportunities for empowerment, joy, and (serious) play. Classrooms are simultaneously subject to political, financial, and structural pressures that can impede our creativity and ability to speculate. The System is vigilant against too much neurodivergent joy and freedom. However, for Liam Semler, creativity can flourish within these limits. Semler describes class as 'Ardenspace': 'a type of dreaming ... creativity provoked by the system' and based on keen awareness of what the system is and how it is operating on us, how we can 'exploit' it and how it enables us.[116] Sarah Amsler and Keri Facer emphasise that, in imagining the future, we must be careful not to foreclose potential futures but keep them open. Writing on the UK education system, they argue that the frameworks we are all living and educating in are designed to resist our urgent attempts to imagine more socially just futures and find alternatives to the status quo. Amsler and Facer write that it is crucial to accept that we cannot predict the future, and to focus on shaping uncertain and non-foreclosed futures in the present.[117]

This final section imagines what a neurodiversity-inclusive Shakespeare studies could look like and feel like, what structures we would need to have in place for it to happen. This future may be nearer than we think. The section is short because most of the work is done by readers' and students' imaginations. Though I concentrated on the end of Jacques' 'seven ages of man' speech, examining earlier points in the life of the man he describes suggests that neurodivergent experience was present before the 'pantaloon'. The soldier, for instance, seems echolalically, neurodivergently, ticcing, 'full of strange oaths' (*As You Like It* II.vii.50). It can be difficult for students to know what to ask for if they haven't first seen, imagined, heard, or read it. I propose

---

[116] Liam Semler, *Teaching Shakespeare and Marlowe* (London: Bloomsbury, 2013), 53.

[117] Sarah Amsler and Keri Facer, 'Contesting Anticipatory Regimes in Education', *Futures* 94 (2017), 6–14.

two exercises to help imagine futures, then end this Element with a toolkit of resources for teaching Shakespeare and neurodiversity so that readers can work towards the inclusive future we want.

Activity: Asking 'What If?'

This Element has posed a series of questions, such as: what if we unleash the autistic joy in the Bastard's repetitions? What if Lear has dementia or BPD? What if theatres and classrooms were totally accessible? What if we read Shakespeare according to the temporalities of ADHD? Educators might ask students to come up with their own 'what ifs', then support them to develop their 'what if . . . ' readings of Shakespeare, with questions such as:

What would that reading look like?
What would the costume be?
How would you stage that?
Which lines would we cut or alter?
How would we perform the lines?
What would be the impact on other characters?
Who benefits from your reading?
Whom is your reading speaking to, and whom does it ignore?

Educators might invite neurodivergent actors into their classrooms to try out multiple neurodivergent interpretations of a given scene or character. In tracing fully the far-reaching effects of neurodivergent readings, students can appreciate these readings' disruptive power and their abilities to offer insights that ripple through a whole text.

Activity: Remodelling the Academy

Educators might tell students they can do *anything* to remodel the institution they learn in, and the closest theatre to them. Students might read work such as (for the UK) Sarah Olive's *Shakespeare Valued*, Michael Dobson's *The Making of the National Poet*, and Joe Falocco's *Reimagining Shakespeare's Playhouse* to understand the ways in which Shakespeare has shaped and formed parts of institutions like the curriculum and the theatre in the country they learn in. Educators could also provide students with documents such as their local theatre, school, or university's statement on disability access, to analyse and annotate with suggestions. Students might take 'sensory tours' or 'access tours' of their institutions, reflecting on what they might be like for people with specific access requirements and/or sensory sensitivities. To prepare for such a tour, students can list the various features of a building that can affect neurodivergent learners: noise levels, temperature, lighting, the availability of quiet spaces, hygiene facilities, and so on. Then, together the students can tour the building, or the classroom if that is easier, and note what they experience: is there a distracting whining noise coming from the radiators, for example? Do corridors funnel students together so that they have to wait for lectures in a big crowd without a space to sit quietly? Are there noisy hand-dryers in the bathrooms? When areas of an institution are inaccessible, it may not be possible for students to even complete their tour; this is useful information in itself. Reflecting on what it is like to journey to the classroom, and what the room is like once they are there, can help students to appreciate which of the material features of their institution are facilitating their learning, and which are obstructing it. Then, students are well placed to answer questions which address Shakespeare's cultural role and status: what is the ideal Shakespeare classroom like? What about the ideal Shakespearean performance space? How do the spaces in which we encounter Shakespeare welcome or marginalise neurodivergent people? Such a discussion can and should be intersectional. As Amrita Dhar writes in her analysis of *Othello*, 'disability is a much broader social, historical, and cultural phenomenon than can be addressed through character-ological or tropological analyses. Disability exists as a matter of climate, mood, setting, epistemology, and environment', which includes not just the built environment but the raced and classed structures of our institutions: 'a junction of twenty-first-century realities in im/migration, first-versus-third-world restrictions of mobility and access, continuing anti-BIPOC racism at multiple levels of our global present, persistent settler-colonialism, systemic ableism, and heteronormative patriarchy'.[118]

---

[118] Amrita Dhar, 'Shakespeare, Race, and Disability: *Othello* and Wheeling Strangers of Here and Everywhere', in Patricia Akhimie, ed., *The Oxford Handbook of Shakespeare and Race* (Oxford: Oxford University Press, 2024) (pp. 171–92), 173.

To support this exercise, educators might set a text like Hamja Ahsan's *Shy Radicals*. In *Shy Radicals*, Ahsan imagines to the full the state of Aspergistan: 'an independent pan-Shyist state representing the interests of all Shy, Introvert, and Autism Spectrum peoples'.[119] Ahsan lists articles of Shyria – Aspergistan's law, designed to protect these peoples' interests and needs against Extrovert Supremacy – and transcribes documents sent between Introvert political actors. The legal articles deal with everything from a ban on strobe lighting, to Aspergistan's national anthem (the sound of a seashell), to the institution of 'quiet police' who come and rescue introverts from noisy social situations, to life-long guaranteed income for independent researchers and several other recommendations for dismantling Extrovert Supremacy in university life.[120] Students might write their own imagined academy, using (as Ahsan does) any number of forms, for example legal articles, an architectural plan, and transcripts of conversations or emails between key actors in the academy. Educators can prompt students to ask, how do we get to this point? What money, friends, people, skills do we need? Do we have them? Who is blocking us from getting to this point? How and why? What information do we need in order to ask for change? Students might borrow an activity from Ahsan (who has held votes, in various locations, on joining Aspergistan) and hold a democratic vote on whether they want to join their imagined academy. They might try and live according to their imagined academy's rules for a given time-period, ranging from a single class to life. They might write a constitution. It might become reality.

Conclusion

This section has explored why literature, and Shakespeare studies as a subset of literature, is important. It is not important because Shakespeare is 'the great bard', the greatest writer to have lived. It is not important because analysing literature gets us money (it generally doesn't). Studying literature is important because it allows us to speculate, to imagine wildly and justly. It is an essential part of a neurodiverse future.

---

[119] Hamja Ahsan, *Shy Radicals: The Antisystemic Politics of the Militant Introvert* (London: Bookworks, 2017), 16.

[120] Ahsan, *Shy Radicals*, 72–74.

Resource Toolkit

Actions: Creating Community and Solidarity

- Help students to set up a neurodiversity group that they are able to lead meaningfully. Give them autonomy over whom they invite to speak, or which activities they want to focus on. If you can, allocate a budget for a students' neurodiversity group which they can use to run events on Shakespeare and neurodivergence or purchase items like headphones and fidget toys for accessibility, attend a relaxed theatre performance, or buy books for a small neurodiversity-and-Shakespeare library.
- Set up events that celebrate neurodiverse achievement and creativity, especially that of students: for instance, a poetry reading by neurodivergent poets.
- Remember the long history of neurodivergent people – make it visible by discussing and teaching it, and having it on the walls.
- Let students know that neurodiversity studies is a serious academic discipline. Use academic texts and classroom exercises to give them the ability to engage with it seriously and rigorously.

Explicitly value neurodivergent ways of reading and interpreting literary texts (like Attias's 'mind-meandering' discussed in Section 2), as critical praxes that have an important place in the classroom.

Reading

A starting point to spark ideas, rather than an exhaustive list.

Ahsan, Hamja, *Shy Radicals: The Antisystemic Politics of the Militant Introvert* (London: Bookworks, 2017).

Kafer, Alison, *Feminist, Queer, Crip* (Bloomington, IN: Indiana University Press, 2013).

Limburg, Joanne, *Letters to My Weird Sisters* (London: Atlantic Books, 2021).

Loftis, Sonya Freeman, *Shakespeare and Disability Studies* (Oxford: Oxford University Press, 2021).

Mitchell, Wendy, *What I Wish People Knew about Dementia: From Someone Who Knows* (London: Bloomsbury, 2022).

Nerenberg, Jenara, *Divergent Mind* (London: HarperOne, 2020).

Omeiza, Kala Allen, *Autistic and Black* (London: Jessica Kingsley, 2024).

Piepzna-Samarasinha, Leah Lakshmi, *Care Work: Dreaming Disability Justice* (Vancouver: Arsenal Pulp Press, 2018).

The Future Is Disabled (Vancouver: Arsenal Pulp Press, 2022).

Price, Margaret, *Mad at School: Rhetorics of Mental Disability and Academic Life* (Ann Arbor, MI: Michigan University Press, 2011).

Purkis, Yenn, and Wenn Lawson, *The Autistic Trans Guide to Life* (London: Jessica Kingsley, 2021).

Schalk, Sami, *Black Disability Politics* (Durham, NC: Duke University Press, 2022).

Stenning, Anna, Hanna Rosqvist, and Nick Chown, eds., *Neurodiversity Studies: A New Critical Paradigm* (London: Routledge, 2020).

Walker, Nick, *Neuroqueer Heresies* (Fort Worth, TX: Autonomous Press, 2021).

Yergeau, Remi, *Authoring Autism* (Durham, NC: Duke University Press, 2017).

Websites

Correct in March 2023

Brooks, René, *Black Girl Lost Keys* https://blackgirllostkeys.com.

Brown, Lydia X. Z., *Autistic Hoya* https://autistichoya.com.

Ingram, Alan, Clark Lawlor, Stuart Sim, et al., *Before Depression* www.beforedepression.com/.

McGillicuddy, Tara, and Lynne Edris, co-hosts *ADHD Support Talk Radio* https://adhdsupporttalk.com/.

Thom, Jess, *Tourettes Hero* www.touretteshero.com/about/.

Walker, Nick, *Neuroqueer: The Writings of Dr Nick Walker* https://neuroqueer.com/.

Wong, Alice, founder, *Disability Visibility Project* https://disabilityvisi
    bilityproject.com/.

Woods, Angela, Charles Fernyhough, Ben Alderson-Day, et al.,
    Hearing the Voice: Interdisciplinary Voice-hearing Research https://
    hearingthevoice.org/.

Acknowledgements

A title like *Shakespeare and Neurodiversity* might look deceptively like a definitive guide, positioning itself as the sole 'explainer' of neurodiversity and Shakespeare. That is far from the truth. Neurodiversity Studies is collaborative; numerous people contribute directly to my understanding of neurodiversity, many of them cited above. Thank you to the series editors Liam Semler and Gillian Woods for this opportunity and their guidance. When I was stuck with Section 4, Katherine Schaap Williams generously invigorated it. The Element was improved by Meredith Knowles' insightful comments. Thank you to everyone who has helped me develop my ideas on neurodivergence and brought brightness to the grind of precarious academic employment, not least Anna Stenning, Louise Creechan, Jenny Bergenmar, Mary Robson, Robert Stagg, Avi Mendelson, and Bridget Escolme. Thank you to everyone I collaborate with on the Neurodiversity at Oxford project; the team, Siân Grønlie, Joel Casey, Alvin Leung, and Georgia Lin, and hundreds of contributors including (the as-yet-unmentioned) Sarah Stephenson-Hunter, Mahlia Amatina, Joanne Limburg, Eulalia D'Souza, Kala Allen Omeiza, G&T Theatre Company, Colin Larkworthy, and Angie Alderman for showing us what neurodivergent wisdom and creativity can do, and to my wife Martha Sofía Franco Rodríguez for her support and encouragement. Thank you to everyone at the *Neurodiversity and the Creative Arts* conference we ran at Birkbeck, University of London in 2020 for excellent pandemic discussions. Thank you most of all to my neurodivergent students.

Cambridge Elements ☰

Shakespeare and Pedagogy

Liam E. Semler
The University of Sydney

Liam E. Semler is Professor of Early Modern Literature in the Department of English at the University of Sydney. He is author of Teaching Shakespeare and Marlowe: Learning versus the System (2013) and co-editor (with Kate Flaherty and Penny Gay) of Teaching Shakespeare beyond the Centre: Australasian Perspectives (2013). He is editor of Coriolanus: A Critical Reader (2021) and co-editor (with Claire Hansen and Jackie Manuel) of Reimagining Shakespeare Education: Teaching and Learning through Collaboration (Cambridge, forthcoming). His most recent book outside Shakespeare studies is The Early Modern Grotesque: English Sources and Documents 1500–1700 (2019). Liam leads the Better Strangers project which hosts the open-access Shakespeare Reloaded website (shakespearereloaded.edu.au).

Gillian Woods
University of Oxford

Gillian Woods is an Associate Professor and Tutorial Fellow in English at Magdalen College, University of Oxford. She is the author of Shakespeare's Unreformed Fictions (2013; joint winner of Shakespeare's Globe Book Award), Romeo and Juliet: A Reader's Guide to Essential Criticism (2012), and numerous articles about Renaissance drama. She is the co-editor (with Sarah Dustagheer) of Stage Directions and Shakespearean Theatre (2018). She is currently working on a new edition of A Midsummer Night's Dream for Cambridge University Press, as well as a Leverhulme-funded monograph about Renaissance Theatricalities. As founding director of the Shakespeare Teachers' Conversations, she runs a seminar series that brings together university academics, school teachers and educationalists from non-traditional sectors, and she regularly runs workshops for schools.

ABOUT THE SERIES

The teaching and learning of Shakespeare around the world is complex and changing. Elements in Shakespeare and Pedagogy synthesises theory and practice, including provocative, original pieces of research, as well as dynamic, practical engagements with learning contexts.

Cambridge Elements ☰

Shakespeare and Pedagogy

ELEMENTS IN THE SERIES

Printed in the United States
by Baker & Taylor Publisher Services